Installing, Upgrading and Troubleshooting

Step by Step Guide, A Complete Guide and Reference

Quick Chapters Overview

DEDICATION PAGE

This book is dedicated to my beloved family members and friends.

ABOUT AUTHOR

The author has been working in the field of information technology in different universities of United States of America. He has been involved in computer imaging processes, deploying security patches for servers, troubleshooting network (LAN, WAN, and Wireless) technologies, fixing hardware and software related issues and documenting them on daily basis, and offering information technology related workshops at different educational institutions. The author holds A+ certification, Network+ certification, and MCTS (Microsoft Certified Technology Specialist) certification in addition to his degree in information technology and minor in Statistics.

TABLE OF CONTENTS

WINDOWS HELP AND SUPPORT

Microsoft users may search for basic *Windows Help and Support* tutorials to enhance knowledge about Windows 7 operating system. To open *Windows Help and Support* window, press *F1* key from a keyboard. Type a keyword in the search box to find tutorials.

RECOMMENDED WINDOWS 7 HARDWARE REQUIREMENTS

Hardware & Software Components	32-bit Operating System	64-bit Operating System
Processor	1 GHz 32-bit Processor	1 GHz 64-bit Processor
Physical Memory (RAM)	1 GB	2GB
Free Hard Disk Space	16 GB	20 GB
Graphics Card	DirectX-9 Graphics Card with WDDM Driver	DirectX-9 Graphics Card with WDDM Driver

Table 1.1: Recommended Windows 7 Hardware Requirements

MICROSOFT WINDOWS 7 - FEATURE COMPARISON

Microsoft Corporation released six versions of Windows 7 edition all over the world. It is recommended to compare and contrast Windows 7 features to purchase a particular version of Microsoft operating system.

The table 1.2 shows comparision of Microsoft Windows 7 versions.

	Starter	Home Basic	Home Premium	Professional	Ultimate	Enterprise
Max Physical RAM (32-bit OS)	4 GB	4 GB	4 GB	4 GB	4 GB	4 GB
Max. Physical RAM (64-bit OS)	NA	NA	16 GB	192 GB	192 GB	192 GB

	Starter	Home Basic	Home Premium	Professional	Ultimate	Enterprise
Max. Physical CPUs Supported	1	1	1	2	2	2
64-bit Processor Support	No	No	No	Yes	Yes	Yes
32/64-bit Versions Support	32-bit only	Both	Both	Both	Both	Both
Fast User Switching	No	Yes	Yes	Yes	Yes	Yes
Desktop Windows Manager	No	Yes	Yes	Yes	Yes	Yes
Multi-Touch	No	No	Yes	Yes	Yes	Yes
Windows Aero	No	No	Yes	Yes	Yes	Yes
Windows Media Center	No	No	Yes	Yes	Yes	Yes
Windows Mobility Center	No	Yes	Yes	Yes	Yes	Yes
PC Network Backup	No	No	No	Yes	Yes	Yes
Windows Backup	Yes	Yes	Yes	Yes	Yes	Yes
AppLocker	No	No	No	No	Yes	Yes
Home Group	Join Only	Join Only	Join and Create	Join and Create	Join and Create	Join and Create
BitLocker Drive Encryption	No	No	No	No	Yes	Yes
Group Policy Support	No	No	No	Yes	Yes	Yes
DVD Playback	No	No	Yes	Yes	Yes	Yes
Remote Desktop	Yes	Yes	Yes	Yes	Yes	Yes

	Starter	Home Basic	Home Premium	Professional	Ultimate	Enterprise
Encrypting File System	No	No	No	Yes	Yes	Yes
Domain Support	No	No	No	Yes	Yes	Yes
Multiple Monitors Support	No	Yes	Yes	Yes	Yes	Yes
Windows XP Mode	No	No	No	Yes	Yes	Yes
Presentation Mode	No	No	No	Yes	Yes	Yes
Virtual Hard Drive Booting	No	No	No	No	Yes	Yes
Windows Anytime Upgrade	Yes	Yes	Yes	Yes	No	No
Windows Flip	Yes	Yes	Yes	Yes	Yes	Yes
Windows Flip - 3D	No	No	Yes	Yes	Yes	Yes
Windows Defender	Yes	Yes	Yes	Yes	Yes	Yes
Parental Controls	Yes	Yes	Yes	Yes	Yes	Yes
Windows ReadyDrive	Yes	Yes	Yes	Yes	Yes	Yes
Windows ReadyBoost	Yes	Yes	Yes	Yes	Yes	Yes
Snipping Tool	No	No	Yes	Yes	Yes	Yes
Sticky Notes	No	No	Yes	Yes	Yes	Yes
Windows Fax and Scan	Yes	Yes	Yes	Yes	Yes	Yes
XPS Viewer	Yes	Yes	Yes	Yes	Yes	Yes
Windows Media Center	No	No	Yes	Yes	Yes	Yes
Windows DVD Maker	No	No	Yes	Yes	Yes	Yes
Sync Center	Yes	Yes	Yes	Yes	Yes	Yes

	Starter	Home Basic	Home Premium	Professional	Ultimate	Enterprise
SMB (Server Message Block) Connections	20	20	20	20	20	20
Network and Sharing Center	Yes	Yes	Yes	Yes	Yes	Yes
IIS Web Server	No	No	Yes	Yes	Yes	Yes
RSS Support	Yes	Yes	Yes	Yes	Yes	Yes
Network Bridge	No	Yes	Yes	Yes	Yes	Yes
Offline Files	No	No	No	Yes	Yes	Yes
Multilingual User Interface (MUI) Language Packs	No	No	No	No	Yes	Yes
Location-aware Printing	No	No	No	Yes	Yes	Yes
Device Stage	Yes	Yes	Yes	Yes	Yes	Yes
Internet Connection Sharing	No	Yes	Yes	Yes	Yes	Yes
DirectAccess	No	No	No	No	Yes	Yes
BranchCache	No	No	No	No	Yes	Yes

Table 1.2: Microsoft Windows 7 - Feature Comparison

WINDOWS 7 UPGRADE PATH

The table 1.3 shows an upgrade path of Windows 7 editions.

Upgrade ➡ ⬇ From To	Windows 7 Starter	Windows 7 Home Basic	Windows 7 Home Premium	Windows 7 Professional	Windows 7 Ultimate
Windows 7 Starter	Clean	Upgrade	Upgrade	Upgrade	Upgrade
Windows 7 Home Basic	Clean	Clean	Upgrade	Upgrade	Upgrade
Windows 7 Home Premium	Clean	Clean	Clean	Upgrade	Upgrade
Windows 7 Professional	Clean	Clean	Clean	Clean	Upgrade
Windows 7 Ultimate	Clean	Clean	Clean	Clean	Clean

Table 1.3: Windows 7 Upgrade Path

UNSUPPORTED MICROSOFT OPERATING SYSTEMS

Microsoft Corporation does not provide an upgrade path for one of the following operating systems.

- Microsoft Windows Vista Starter Edition
- Microsoft Windows Vista Home Basic
- Microsoft Windows XP (All Editions)
- Microsoft Windows Millennium, Microsoft Windows NT 4.0 or Earlier Versions
- Windows NT Server 4.0
- Microsoft Windows 95/98
- Windows 2000/2003/2008 Server

All of the above *Operating Systems* require a custom installation.

32-BIT UPGRADE PATH VERSES 64-BIT UPGRADE PATH

To check system configuration of a machine, click *Start* button to type *System* in the search field (located at left-bottom of the desktop) and then select *System Information* from programs list. In the *System* window, check the system type of a machine from *System* section. In most cases, 32-bit and 64-bit operating systems can be installed on 86-bit CPU and 64-bit CPU, respectively. However, a 32-bit operating system can be installed on a machine that has a 64-bit processor; on the other hand a 64-bit operating system cannot be installed on a 32-bit processor machine.

WINDOWS 7 CLEAN INSTALLATION VERSUS WINDOWS 7 UPGRADE INSTALLATION

The table 1.4 and table 1.5 show an upgrade path of Microsoft Windows XP/Vista/9X/2000 and Microsoft Windows 7. There is no upgrade path available from 32-bit version to 64-bit version of operating systems.

From To ➡ ⬇	Windows 7 Starter	Windows 7 Home Premium	Windows 7 Professional	Windows 7 Ultimate	Windows 7 Enterprise
Windows XP (all editions)	Clean Install	Clean Install	Clean Install	Clean Install	Clean Install
Windows Vista Starter	Clean Install	Clean Install	Clean Install	Clean Install	Clean Install
Windows Vista Home Basic	Clean Install	Upgrade	Clean Install	Upgrade	Clean Install
Windows Vista Home Premium	Clean Install	Upgrade	Clean Install	Upgrade	Clean Install
Windows Vista Business	Clean Install	Clean Install	Upgrade	Upgrade	Upgrade
Windows Vista Ultimate	Clean Install	Clean Install	Clean Install	Upgrade	Clean Install

Windows Vista Enterprise	Clean Install	Clean Install	Clean Install	Clean Install	Upgrade
Windows 9X/2000	Clean Install	Clean Install	Clean Install	Clean Install	Clean Install

Table 1.4: 32-bit Operating Systems Upgrade Path

The table 1.5 shows 64-bit operating systems upgrade path.

From To ➡	Win 7 Starter	Win 7 Home Premium	Win 7 Professional	Win 7 Ultimate	Win 7 Enterprise
Windows XP (all editions)	Clean Install	Clean Install	Clean Install	Clean Install	Clean Install
Windows Vista Starter	Clean Install	Clean Install	Clean Install	Clean Install	Clean Install
Windows Vista Home Basic	Clean Install	Upgrade	Clean Install	Upgrade	Clean Install
Windows Vista Home Premium	Clean Install	Upgrade	Clean Install	Upgrade	Clean Install
Windows Vista Business	Clean Install	Clean Install	Upgrade	Upgrade	Upgrade
Windows Vista Ultimate	Clean Install	Clean Install	Clean Install	Upgrade	Clean Install
Windows Vista Enterprise	Clean Install	Clean Install	Clean Install	Clean Install	Upgrade
Windows 9X/2000	Clean Install	Clean Install	Clean Install	Clean Install	Clean Install

Table 1.5: 64-bit Operating Systems Upgrade Path

WINDOWS 7 UPGRADE ADVISOR

Windows 7 Upgrade Advisor is a free program available to download from Microsoft website. It identifies currently installed hardware and software configurations of a system to see if a personal computer is ready to be upgraded to Windows 7. To download ***Upgrade Advisor*** utility, type the following ***URL*** (***Universal Resource Locator***) in Internet Explorer browser, http://www.microsoft.com/downloads/details.aspx?display lang=en&FamilyID=1b544e90-7659-4bd9-9e51-2497c146af15 (a live link at the time of writing this book) and then click on ***Download*** to install a copy of ***Windows 7 Upgrade Advisor*** to verify hardware and software system requirements. ***Windows 7 Upgrade Advisor*** can also be downloaded by searching or typing these keywords (***Microsoft Windows 7 upgrade advisor download)*** by going to the www.google.com search engine.

User must perform following steps to install ***Windows 7 Upgrade Advisor***.

- User will be asked to either save or run this file. Click on ***Save***, if user would like to save ***Windows 7 Upgrade Advisor*** file for later use, otherwise click on ***Run*** to install upgrade advisor. This process may take few minutes to run this program.

- Click on ***Run*** to extract the content of this program.

- From ***Windows 7 Upgrade Advisor Setup*** wizard, read Microsoft license terms and conditions to install this software. If you, as a user, agree to their license terms and conditions, click on ***I accept the license terms*** and then click on ***Install***. If you do not agree to their license terms and conditions, click on ***I do not accept the license terms*** and then click on ***Cancel***. If you do not accept this license agreement, installation process will stop here. Installation process may take several minutes to complete.

- By default, ***Windows 7 Upgrade Advisor*** program will be launched after clicking on ***Close*** button. If user would like to launch this program later, clear the ***Launch Windows 7 Upgrade Advisor*** checkbox.

- Click on ***Start Check*** to see if user's PC is ready to be upgrade to Windows 7.

- *Windows Upgrade Advisor* may take several minutes to compile a hardware and software compatibility report. User must take necessary steps to fix any upgrade issues as needed. The report can be saved or printed off by clicking on the *Save Report* button and *Print* button respectively.

WINDOWS 7 CLEAN INSTALLATION

To install a clean copy of Windows 7 on a user machine, insert the Windows 7 DVD disk into the DVD ROM and then reboot/restart the system. System may recognize DVD disk by itself, if not, reboot your machine. Press *F12* key (from a keyboard) as soon as computer starts to force user system to boot from DVD ROM. In most computer systems, *F12* (located at top of a standard keyboard) is the key to enter boot menu to make a boot selection. Function keys (F1, F2, F10, Delete, and Ese) may be designated to enter to boot menu.

Once the DVD disk is recognized by a DVD ROM, user is required to perform following steps to either install a clean copy of Windows 7 or an upgrade copy of Windows 7.

- User will be asked to press any key to install Windows 7. Press any key to continue installing Windows 7.

- Adjust the *language to install*, *time and currency format*, and *keyboard or input method* preferences and then click *Next* to continue.

- Click on *Install now* to continue installing Windows. If user would like to review hardware and operating system specifications, click on *What to know before installing Windows*.

- Windows may take several minutes to copy necessary Windows installation files.

- Enter the product key that came with the system and then click on *Next* to continue installing operating system.

- Click on *Read our privacy statement* if necessary

- Read and accept license terms and conditions and then click on *Next*.

At this point, user is asked to either perform a *Custom* or an *Upgrade* Windows 7 installation. Both options are explained in detail to choose a preferable installation process.

- Select *Custom (advanced)* option to continue installing a clean copy of Windows 7. This option does not keep user's personal data, files, folders, and program settings that are currently installed on a machine.

- Select an *Upgrade* option to continue upgrading a system to *Microsoft Windows 7* from an older version of a *Microsoft Windows XP or Vista* edition. An upgrade process keeps computer files, settings, and programs but it is recommended to have a complete PC backup, in case system crashes during an upgrade process.

If user decides to choose an upgrade option, system may take several minutes to detect and generate a potential issue report. Review the compatibility report carefully before continuing Windows installation process to the next level. Click on *Next* to continue Windows installation.

- If hard-drive has multiple partitions, select a designated partition to install Windows and then click on *Next*.

- Computer manufactures may have multiple pre-installed hard-disk partitions for a system, one partition may be designated to save system files and others may be reserved to save user's personal data.

- Windows will install necessary files to run operating system. This process may take several hours to copy windows files, expanding files, installing features, installing updates, and completing upgrade installation process. System may restart itself several times during Windows 7 installation process.

- User will be asked to create a username for Windows 7 account. Enter a preferable username that is easy to remember.

- The system will suggest a computer name, either keep the suggested computer name created by the system or re-name it according to the user preferences. To continue installation process to the next level, click on *Next*.

- Create a password that must meet complexity requirements as given below and then click on *Next* to continue.

  o Should not use user's account name.

  o Should not use two consecutive characters that is part of the user's full name.

  o Should have at-least six characters length password.

  o Should contain at-least one uppercase character (A through Z), at-least one lowercase character (a through z), at-least one digit (0 through 9), or at-least one non-alphabetic character (!, @, #. $, %, ^, &, *, etc).

- Choose one of the following Windows updates options to continue.

- *Use recommended settings*: The system will install important and recommended updates on a system. If user decides to choose this option then system turns on following features automatically:

  o *Windows automatic updating*: The important and recommended updates will be installed.

  o *Enhanced spyware protection*: A spyware program, *Windows Defender*, protects user profile against spywares. The system downloads and installs *Windows Defender* updates on regular basis to enhance system security against malicious spywares.

  o *Windows problem reporting*: The Windows 7 has *Microsoft Error Reporting* tool that sends necessary information to Microsoft to identify the cause of a problem. If the solution of a problem already exists, the solution will be presented to user to fix the issue that user having with his system.

- o ***Driver from Windows updates***: Windows 7 is capable of downloading and installing device drivers automatically. If the device drivers are available online, it will be downloaded and installed automatically on the user machine.

- o ***Internet Explorer Phishing Filter***: Phishing filter checks against spam websites.

- ***Install important updates only***: Only important updates will be installed on the user system.

- ***Ask me later***: If user decides to choose this option, user machine might not be protected against security threats. Microsoft does not recommend users to enable this option.

- It is recommended to choose ***Use recommended settings*** option to protect system against security threads in computing industry.

- Review time and date settings and then click on ***Next***.

- Select a network location. A public network may be available at an airport, at a coffee shop, or at any other locations where a security key is not required to connect to the Internet. A private network is known to be more secure network which passes encrypted communication across the network. If user is concered of his computer security, private network will be the best choice for the user machine. Select one of the available network locations to continue.

- If user decides to connect to a home network, this process may take several minutes to perform necessary operations to setup a home network.

- If user was successful to connect with a home network, user will be asked to create a homegroup to share pictures, videos, documents, music, and printers. Make a note of homegroup password that might be helpful to connect and share local resources with other local system users.

- Windows might take few minutes to apply appropriate system settings. User's machine must not be turned off forcefully until Windows updates are updated successfully.

WINDOWS 7 ACTIVATION

Click the *Start* button. Right click on *Computer* to choose *Properties* option. From right panel of the *system window*, scroll down to *Windows activation* section to click on X *days until automatic activation. Activate Windows now* link.

Click on *Activate Windows online now* link to activate Microsoft 7 operating system. In order to activate Windows online, user is required to have an Internet connection at the time of Windows activation. If user is not connected with the Internet at the time of Windows activation, user must use phone system to activate the copy of Windows 7.

Windows will take few seconds to activate it. Once the activation is done, successful activation message will confirm the product activation.

ADVANCED DRIVE OPTIONS

Insert the Windows 7 DVD disk into a DVD ROM and then reboot/restart the system. Computer will detect the DVD disk by itself and will start downloading Windows files from the DVD disk. This process may take several minutes downloading Windows system files.

If system did not detect the DVD disk by itself, reboot machine. Press *F12* key (from a keyboard) as soon as computer starts to make a boot order selection. In most computer systems, *F12* (located at top of a standard keyboard) is the key to enter boot menu to make a boot selection. Function keys (F1, F2, F10, Delete, and Ese) may be designated to enter boot menu.

Once the DVD disk is recognized by a DVD ROM, user is required to perform following steps:

- User will be asked to press any key to install Windows 7. Press any key to continue installing Windows 7.
- Adjust the *language to install, time and currency format*, and *keyboard or input method* preferences and then click on *Next* to continue.
- If user would like to review hardware specifications, click on *What to know*

before installing Windows. Click on ***Install now*** to continue installing Windows.

- Enter the product key that came with the system and then click on ***Next*** to continue installing operating system. If user would like to read the privacy statement, click on ***Read our privacy statement***.

- Read and accept license terms and conditions and then click on ***Next***.

- Choose ***Custom (advanced)*** option.

  Select a disk partition and then click on the ***Drive options (advanced)*** to perform one of the following steps to either load device drive, to create/delete hard drive partition(s) and to format/extend hard drive partition(s).

LOAD HARD DISK DRIVER

If hard-drive partition(s) are not visible while installing ***Microsoft Windows 7*** operating system. Hard-disk drivers are necessary to install, click on ***Load Driver*** option to load disk drivers.

Click on ***Browse*** button, select the drive volume that has device driver in it and then click on ***OK***. System may take few minutes to install hard-disk drivers. Reboot machine after installing latest device driver. If user is unable to see any hard-disk partition(s), repeat above steps to install hard-disk drivers again.

CREATE HARD DISK VOLUME/PARTITION

To create new hard-disk volume/partition, user must have unallocated space available. Click on designated unallocated disk space to create new volume/partition and then click on ***New***. Type new hard-disk volume size and then click on ***Apply*** to create a new disk partition. This process may take few minutes to complete.

FORMAT HARD DISK PARTITION

Click the partition that user wants to format and then click on ***Format***. This process may take several minutes to complete. Click ***OK*** to allow disk partition to be formatted. User cannot format an unallocated space disk.

EXTEND HARD DISK PARTITION

To extend a hard-disk partition, select a desire partition and then click on *Extend*. Type new extended volume size and then click on *Apply* to create a new extended system volume.

Click *OK* to continue the process of extending the hard-disk partition. Extending a partition is not a reversible process.

DELETE HARD DISK VOLUME/PARTITION

Select the hard-disk partition that user desires to delete and then click on *Delete* option. Click on *OK* to continue the process of deleting hard-disk partition. It is recommended to have a complete backup of hard-drive partition before deleting it.

IMPROVE SYSTEM PERFORMANCE

Everyone likes to have a faster computer to shop online, play online games, apply for a college admission and in today's world even you have option to renew your driver license online.

Running a spyware scan and a virus scan may improve the performance of a computer. It is recommended to install a paid or a free version of antivirus/antispyware program to protect your computer against virus and spywares. User must run antivirus/anti-spyware scan once in a week to removes unnecessary files out of a computer to make the system run faster. A list of recommended antivirus/antispyware software is listed below. To download any of following listed programs, go to a search engine (e.g., www.ask.com, www.yahoo.com, www.google.com, etc) to type in software name to get a live downloadable link.

List of Free Antivirus Programs:

- Avast Antivirus
- AVG Antivirus
- Avira Antivirus Personal
- FortiClient Security Essentials

- Panda Cloud Antivirus
- Spyware Doctor with Antivirus (Download Google Pack)
- Threatfire
- Trend Micro HouseCall

The above listed antivirus program may ask you to provide personal information (e.g., your name and email address) for registration purpose. Credit card information should not be disclosed to any of the above listed anti-virus vendors unless you wanted to upgrade the program from a free version to a full version. They should never ask you for credit card information.

List of Free Antispyware Programs:

- A-Squared
- Advanced Windows Care
- Arovax Antispyware
- CWShredder
- MalwareBytes Anti-Malware
- Windows Defender
- Spybot Search & Destroy
- Spyware Blaster
- Spyware Terminator
- Super AntiSpyware
- ThreatExpert

The above antivirus/antispyware programs are free to install on a system. It is recommended reading online reviews about an antivirus/antispyware program to check pros and corns of that program. Reviews are written by home users, business users, industrial users, and enterprise professionals to help new users to install a recommended antivirus/antispyware program. Reviews can be found by typing the name of the antivirus program in www.google.com. Make sure to add a keyword (***reviews)*** at end of each search.

If system still running slow after scanning your computer with an antivirus/ antispyware program, you might have one of the following problems with your system. I would not recommend you to replace any computer parts by yourself unless you title yourself a computer technician.

- Bad Memory/ Low Memory
- Bad Hard Drive/ Low Hard Drive Space
- Bad Motherboard
- Bad Power Supply

Take your system to any nearby computer store to replace any parts which may be causing your computer to run slow. If one part of your computer is getting bad that might degrade system performance. For example, if a CD-ROM of your system is bad that might cause your computer to boot slow.

GETTING STARTED WITH WINDOWS 7

Getting Started panel combines a list of necessary programs to help users to configure their systems properly. Panel includes:

- Introduction of Windows 7

- Add new user's accounts

- Make screen text font appear bigger or smaller

- Transfer files and settings from an older system to newer system

OPEN GETTING STARTED WINDOW

To open *Getting started* window:

- Open *Control Panel*

- By default, control panel items are set to view by category. To view *all control panel items* list, choose *Large icons* or *Small icons* option from drop down menu of *View by* list (located at top-right side of the control panel).

- Double-click on *Getting Started* icon

Image 2.1: Control Panel - Larger Icons

DESKTOP PREVIEW

Desktop preview feature introduced with Windows 7 to minimize or maximize all currently running window's applications instantly. To minimize or maximize windows applications, place the mouse cursor at end of the *taskbar*.

Image 2.2: Desktop Preview

ACTION CENTER

Action Center window is divided into two sections, *Security and Maintenance*, to monitor security threats against virus and spyware attacks. The *action center* window resolves personal backup issues of a computer and user will be notified on daily basis to perform windows updates to download latest antivirus/spyware definitions, if needed.

For example, if a system does not detect anti-virus program that must be installed and updated on a machine to provide maximum security to a system. The system will prompt an alert to inform user to install the necessary software to provide maximum system security against virus attacks. The security messages can be turned off by clicking on hyperlink *Turn off messages about virus protection*. The security software list can be viewed by clicking on toggle button (located at far right side of the security section).

To open *Action Center*, open *All Control Panels Items* and then scroll down to *Action Center* to open it.

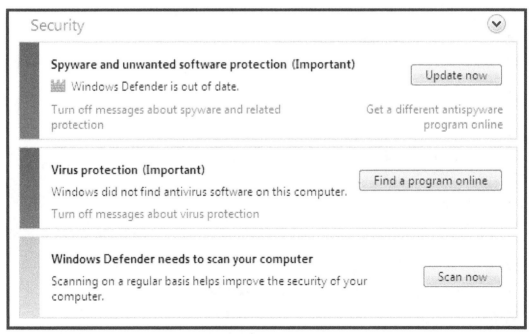

Image 2.3: Action Center - Security Section

System administrators can turn on or off applicable security messages by clicking on the hyperlink *Turn off messages about…..*

In the *Maintenance* section, user has option to analyze problem/solution reports, set up and verify *Windows Backup*, check and install *Windows updates*. Also, it adds *troubleshooting* (*Programs*, *Hardware and Sound*, *Network and Internet*, *Appearance and Personalization* and *System and Security*) section and *recovery* section to perform necessary maintenance on a system.

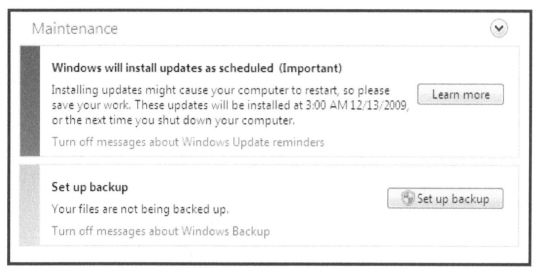

Image 2.4: Action Center - Maintenance Section

To change troubleshooting settings, click on toggle button to view maintenance options list and then click on *Change troubleshooting settings* link to view and adjust preferable settings.

The automatic computer maintenance can be turned off by clicking on *Off* option from the *Computer Maintenance* section. The *other settings* can be adjusted by checking off one of the following options.

- *Allow users to browse for troubleshooters available from the Windows Online Troubleshooting service*
- *Allow troubleshooting to begin immediately when started*

Click on *OK* to change troubleshooting settings.

NOTIFICATION AREA CUSTOMIZATION

Right click on the taskbar to choose *Properties* option from the list. From *Taskbar and Start Menu Properties* window, under the *Taskbar* tab, click on **Customize...** button to adjust notification area preferences.

The icons behavior can be adjusted to:

- *Show icon and notifications*
- *Hide icon and notifications*
- *Only show notifications*

Select any of the above listed icon behaviors and then click **OK** to save changes. Icon behavior changes can revert to default settings by clicking on **Restore default icon behaviors**. If all system icons are required to be visible on notification area, check **Always show all icons and notifications on the taskbar** option.

The system icons can be turned on or off to customize notifications area. Click on *Turn system* icons on or off link to adjust preferences. From *System Icon* window, set appropriate system icons behaviors and then click on *OK* to save changes.

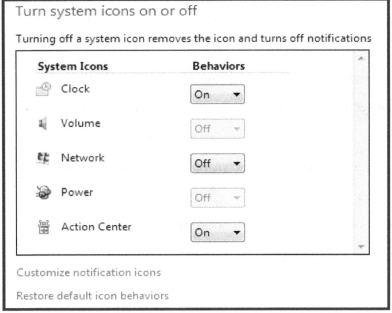

Image 2.5: Customize Notification Icons

WINDOWS EXPERIENCE INDEX SCORE

The *Windows Experience Index* (WEI) score measures computer hardware components performance which includes *Processor, Memory (RAM), Graphics Card, Gamming Graphics, and Primary Hard Disk*. The system performance base score is rated between 1, least possible base score, and 7.9 best possible base score, for a system. The *base score* of a system is determined by the lowest sub score of the weakest computer component. The WEI base score table measures the cumulative performance of a system hardware and software configurations. The performance of a system may be improved by replacing the computer component that has least sub score rating.

NAVIGATE WINDOWS EXPERIENCE INDEX (WEI) BASE SCORE TABLE

To navigate *Windows Experience Index Base Score* table:

- Open *Control Panel*.
- From drop down menu of *view by*, choose *small icons* option to view all components of *Control Panel*.
- From *All Control Panel Items* **window,** Double-click *Performance Information and Tools* link to open the WEI window.

BITLOCKER DRIVE ENCRYPTION

BitLocker drive encryption was introduced with Windows Vista operating system to enhance data security by encrypting the user's system drive. A proper authentication key is required to access encrypted hard drive contents. The BitLocker encryption key may be saved in a USB drive or in the system drive (by default, *C* (system drive) drive is designated to keep Windows operating system files) or in BIOS (*Basic Input Output System*) of a machine. BitLocker drive encryption feature is available in *Windows 7 Ultimate, Windows 7 Enterprise* and *Windows Server 2008* operating systems.

BITLOCKER DRIVE ENCRYPTION REQUIREMENTS

- At-least two hard drive partitions are required; one partition saves system start-up files and other partitions save encrypted data to protect data privacy.

- System hard drive partitions must be formatted with *NTFS (New Technology File System)*.

- System *BIOS* must be compatible with *Trusted Platform Module* (TPM) and it must support USB devices at start-up of a computer. If TPM and USB devices are not supported at the start-up of a computer, computer *BIOS* needs to be upgraded.

- Requires TPM version 1.2 or higher micro chip to enhance hardware authentication to protect data privacy. BitLocker will store cryptographic keys in the TPM and stored keys can only be decrypted by TPM to minimize the data theft risk.

If system is not TPM compatible to store cryptographic keys, a removable USB device may be used to store keys.

TURN ON BITLOCKER DRIVE ENCRYPTION

To open *BitLocker Drive Encryption Tool*:

- Open *All Control Panel Items*
- Click on *BitLocker Drive Encryption*
- Click on *Turn On BitLocker*

Image 2.6: Turn on BitLocker

If TPM is not present on a user machine, an error will be prompted.

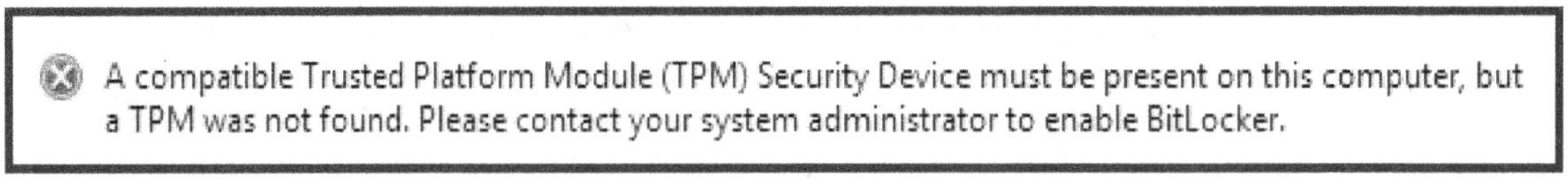

 A compatible Trusted Platform Module (TPM) Security Device must be present on this computer, but a TPM was not found. Please contact your system administrator to enable BitLocker.

Image 2.7: Trusted Platform Module Security Device Error

If system meets BitLocker requirements; user will be asked to either unlock the drive by entering a password or by using a smart card. Advanced users may use smart card to unlock the drive.

Image 2.8: BitLocker Drive Encryption - Password and Smart Card

Enter a password that is easily to remember and it must include uppercase letters, lowercase letters, numbers, spaces and symbols. Click on *Next* button to continue setting up BitLocker drive encryption.

Once the password is entered successfully, either save recovery key in a USB drive or print off recovery key. Users are recommended to use both options to save recovery key.

Click on *Next* after saving recovery key. To encrypt a system drive, click on the *Start Encrypting* button. Encryption process may take few minutes to few hours depending on the size of a computer hard-drive and speed of the processor. User may *Pause* encrypting process at any time and resume it at later time.

MANAGE BITLOCKER DRIVE ENCRYPTION

Choose *Manage BitLocker* option by right-clicking on the encrypted drive to select one of the following options to manage a drive.

- Change password to unlock the drive
  - Set a new password if old password is compromised.
- Remove password from this drive
  - If user does not desire to make this drive password protected anymore, click on this option to remove the password. User may be asked to provide old password to remove the current password.
- Add a smart card to unlock the drive
  - Choose this option to add a smart card to unlock this drive.
- Save or print recovery key again
  - The recovery key can be reprinted or saved by choosing this option.
- Automatically unlock this drive on this computer
  - If this option is enabled, the drive will be unlocked on this computer without asking user to enter a password.

READY BOOST DEVICE

Windows 7 is capable of adding non-volatile flash/USB memory without adding a physical memory chip onto the motherboard. The *Ready Boost* device increases the performance of a system by storing file cache on a USB drive. The device must have:

- At-least USB 2.0 type
- Must have at-least 256 MB in size
- Should have access time of 1ms or less
- Must support NTFS, FAT16, and FAT32 formats
- Minimum of 2.5 MB/s for 4 KB random READ speed
- Minimum of 1.75 MB/s for 512 KB random WRITE speed
- Must have at-least 235 MB of free space

The question arises, how would a user verifies the ready boost drive requirements? Plug the USB device into a computer, by default an *auto play* window will pop-up, click on *Speed up my system* icon from the *General options* section.

The USB drive properties dialog box is open, click on *ReadyBoost* tab to select *Use this device* option. Under the *Use this device* section, system speed can be reserved by moving the slider right or left to increase or decrease the space, respectively. Click on *Apply* and then click *OK* to save *Ready Boost* drive preferences.

BASIC SYSTEM INFORMATION

To view basic system information:

- Open *All Control Panel Items*
- Open *System* to view basic computer information

RUN COMMAND WINDOW

A run command is a dialog box to access computer utilities such as a DOS window, task manager, control panel, network and sharing center, device manager, etc. by typing a command line.

To quickly open a *run command* dialog box, press *Windows Key* and *R* (letter *R* from keyboard) simultaneously. To manually open a *Run Command* dialog box, click on *Start* button to type *run* (this is a command line to open dialog box) in the search bar and then press *Enter* from the keyboard. Type the name of a program or a folder or a document or an Internet resource that a user desires to open by typing a command line in the search bar. For example, if user would like to open a DOS-window, type *cmd* command line in the search bar and then press *Enter* from keyboard to open a DOS-window.

ADD RUN COMMAND IN START MENU

Right-click on *Start* button and then choose *Properties* option from the list. From the *Taskbar and Start Menu Properties* window, click on *Customize* button. Scroll down the list to navigate *Run command* option. To enable this feature, check the *Run command* option to activate it. Click *OK* to save preferences.

WINDOWS DVD MAKER

Windows DVD Maker enables Windows 7 users to create and/or customize videos files, picture files and audio files. *Microsoft Windows 7 Starter* and *Microsoft Windows 7 Home Basic* do not support *Windows DVD Maker* program.

OPEN WINDOWS DVD MAKER

To open *Windows DVD Maker* program, click *Start* button, click *All Programs* and then click *Windows DVD Maker*.

BURN A DVD

Insert a *DVD Disk* into a *DVD ROM*. Open *Windows DVD Maker* program. A welcome screen may be presented, click on *Choose Photos and Videos* to move to the DVD program.

To add a file or a folder into a DVD, click on *Add items* option (from the command bar of the *DVD Maker* window) to add items that needs to be burned into a *DVD disk*. Type disc title (located at bottom of the window) and then click on *Next*.

The *Windows DVD Maker* customizes DVD preferences by selecting available options form *DVD Maker* command bar. Once the preferences are set, click on *Burn* button and then follow on-screen instructions to burn a *DVD*. This process may take several minutes.

Image 2.9: DVD Burner Command Bar

DVD OPTIONS

Open *Windows DVD Maker* program. From detailed pane of *Windows DVD Maker,* click on *Options* to set DVD preferences.

- Choose DVD playback settings. The options are: 1- Start with DVD menu, 2- Play video and end with DVD menu, 3- Play video in a continuous loop
- DVD aspect ratio settings. The options are: 4:3 ratio and 16:9 ratio

- Video format settings. The options are: NTSC and PAL

- DVD burner speed. The options are: Slow, Medium, and Fastest

- Temporary File Location: Click on Browse button to select a temporary file location

Click **OK** to save *DVD* preferences.

OPEN HARDWARE AND SOUND APPLET

To open **Hardware and Sound** applet:

- Open **Control Panel**, and

- Click **Hardware and Sound**

ADJUST SOUND VOLUME

Open **Hardware and Sound** applet. Navigate to the **Sound** icon to click on **Adjust system volume** link.

To adjust speaker volume, move the device slider or an application slider up or down to increase or decrease the volume, respectively. The volume can be muted by clicking on the speaker icon (located at bottom of each device).

SETUP SOUND SYSTEM

Open **Hardware and Sound** applet. Navigate to the **Sound** icon to open **Manage audio devices** link to modify playback device settings. From the **Sound** window, select a speaker type to modify its settings. Click on **Configure** button to start configuring sound system settings.

From **Speaker Setup** window, select computer speaker's audio channels and then click on **Next**. To test speakers, click on **Test** to see if the speakers are connected properly with the system. If the speakers are connected properly, user must hear a sound from speakers system. Click on **Next** to continue and then click on **Finish** to apply audio device settings.

ADJUST SOUND THEME

To adjust sound theme, click *Sounds* tab from *Sound* window. To apply sound effect on a program, first select a sound scheme from drop down menu of the *Sound Scheme* and then select a program from *Program Events* section. To test sound effect of a program event, click on *Test* button. Click on *Apply* and then click *OK* to save sound theme preferences.

CHANGE DESKTOP BACKGROUND

To change desktop background theme:

- Open *All Control Panel Items*.

- Navigate to *Personalization* icon to open it.

- From *Personalization* window, select *Desktop Background* icon (located at bottom of the window) to adjust desktop background settings.

- From drop down menu of *Picture Library*, choose a picture location.

- Select a picture position by clicking on *Picture position* drop down menu.

- If user would like to change desktop theme every X minutes, adjust the preferable times and then click on *OK* to save desktop background preferences.

COMPUTER THEME CUSTOMIZATION

A computer theme customizes the visuals and sounds settings of a system. To customize a computer theme, open *Personalization* window by going to *All Control Panel Items*. *Aero Themes* (if system supports) and *Basic and High Contrast Themes* (most system supports) are availables to customize computer themes. Choose an appropiate theme and then click *OK* to save computer theme settings.

CHANGE WINDOW COLOR AND APPEARANCE

Open *Personalization* window by going to *All Control Panel Items*. Click on *Window Color* to change window's borders, *Start menu* and *taskbar* colors.

SCREEN SAVER CUSTOMIZATION

A screen saver covers computer screen with a picture or an animation whenever user machine is in idle state. To customize a screen saver, open *Personalization* window by going to *All Control Panel Items*. Click on *Screen Saver* (located at bottom of the window) to adjust screen saver settings. From *Screen Saver Settings* dialog box, select *3D Text* screen saver option from *Screen Saver* drop down menu and then click on *Settings*.

To personalize computer screen saver settings, fill out the *text*, *motion*, and *surface style* sections and then click *OK* to save changes. If user does not desire to set any screen saver for his system, choose *None* option from *Screen saver* drop down menu.

ADJUST SCREEN RESOLUTION

Open *Hardware and Sound* applet by going to the *Control panel*. In the *Hardware and Sound* window, click *Adjust screen resolution* link from *Display* section.

To adjust best monitor display color:

- Adjust preferable resolution.
- Click on *Apply* and then click *OK* to save display settings.

REFRESH SCREEN RATE

Open *Hardware and Sound* applet by going to the *Control panel*. In the *Hardware and Sound* window, click *Adjust screen resolution* link from *Display* section. From *Screen Resolution* dialog box, click on *Advanced Settings* button to adjust display settings.

In the *Monitor* tab, from the *Monitor Settings* section choose screen refresh rate from drop down menu of the *Screen refresh rate*. At-least 32 bit or higher color scheme must be selected if this option is available for a system. Click on *Apply* and then click *OK* to save changes.

ADJUST FONT SIZE (DPI)

DPI stands for *dots per inches* and it measures printing or display resolution. To adjust system font size, open *Hardware and Sound* applet from *Control panel*. In the *Hardware and Sound* window, navigate to *Display* icon. From left navigation pane of the *Display*, click on *Set Custom Text Size (DPI)* link to modify DPI settings.

By default, windows screen scale is 100 DPI and larger scale (125, 150, 200 DPIs) options are available to make text font appear bigger on a computer screen.

Select a percentage from drop down menu of *Scale to this percentage of normal size* and then click *OK* to save DPI settings.

MOUSE BUTTON CONFIGURATION

To configure a mouse button, open *Mouse* window by going to the *All Control Panel Items*. In the *Buttons* tab, under the *Button configuration* section, select this option, *Switch primary and secondary buttons,* to change mouse button configuration. Click on *Apply* and then click *OK* to save the mouse configurations.

MOUSE CLICKLOCK CONFIGURATION

From *Mouse Properties* window, click *Buttons* tab. From the *Clicklock* section select this option, *Turn on Clicklock*, to activate mouse clicklock. By default, clicklock is disabled. Once clicklock is enabled, objects such as a file, a folder, or any application shortcuts are drag able without holding down the mouse button. User is required to press left mouse button for less than 5 seconds to activate clicklock and then it will allow user to move an object within a local user account. Click on *Apply* and then click *OK* to save changes. Advanced clicklock settings can be configured by clicking on *Settings* from the *Clicklock* section.

MOUSE POINTER CONFIGURATION

To configure the mouse pointer, open *Mouse Properties* window. From *Mouse Properties* window, click *Pointers* tab and then select a cursor from the *Customize* box.

If user wants a customized cursor that is not a part of the system yet, click on *Browse* button to upload customized cursor and then navigate to that folder in which the customized cursor is saved. Click on *Apply* and then click *OK* to save mouse pointer configurations.

VISIBILITY OF MOUSE CURSOR

From *Mouse Properties* window, click *Pointer Options* tab, under the *Visibility* section, select this option, *Show location of the pointer when I press the CTRL key* to activate visibility of mouse cursor. By default, this option is disabled. It is recommended to enable this option for those users who are low in vision and are having hard time finding mouse cursor. A big round circle will appear on location of the pointer once user press and release the *Ctrl* key (located at most left-bottom of a standard keyboard). Click on *Apply* and then click *OK* to save mouse cursor preferences.

PROGRAMS AND FEATURES

Programs and Features is an administrator tool to delete, modify, install and manage programs, and view Windows updates history.

UNINSTALL A PROGRAM

To uninstall a program, open *Programs and Features* applet by going to *All Control Panel Items*.

Select an application that user wishes to remove and then click *Uninstall* option from the command bar. A user may be asked to provide administrative credentials to perform this task.

VIEW INSTALLED WINDOWS UPDATES

To view installed Windows updates, open *Programs and Features* applet by going to *All Control Panel Items*. From left navigation panel, click *View installed updates* link. To remove a windows update, highlight an update that needs to be uninstalled and then click on *Uninstall* option from the command bar.

WINDOWS - HIDDEN PROGRAMS AND FEATURES

The *Windows Programs and Features* are pre-loaded windows programs to install on a machine as needed.

OPEN WINDOWS PROGRAMS AND FEATURES

To open *Programs and Features* template:

- Open *Control Panel*
- Sort out *Control Panel Items* by *Category*
- Open *Programs* link
- Click on *Turn Windows features on or off* link from *Programs and Features* section

Image 2.10: Programs and Features

To turn on *Windows Hidden Features*, select an appropriate application that user would like to install on a machine and then click *OK* to perform installation. Turning on or off a window's feature may take several minutes to complete the process. Follow on-screen instructions to install pre-loaded hidden programs.

WINDOWS UPDATES

- Open *All Control Panel Items* window.
- To check system updates, click on *Check for updates* link from left navigation panel of the *Windows update*.
- To download latest Windows updates, click on *Install Updates* button from right navigation panel. It may take several minutes downloading and installing latest system updates. If Windows updates are installed successfully, user will be notified. A cold re-boot is required to apply changes to a machine.

WINDOWS UPDATES SETTINGS

To open *Windows Updates* settings:

- Click on *Start* button

- Click on *Control Panel*

- Click on *All Control Panel Items* (this steps might not be necessary)

- Click on *Windows Updates*

- Click on *Change Settings* from left navigation panel

- Adjust appropriate *Windows Updates* settings

- Click *OK* to save settings.

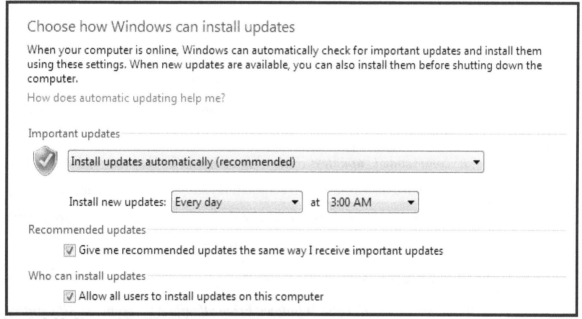

Image 2.11: Choose how Windows can install updates

VIEW WINDOWS UPDATES HISTORY

To view *Windows Updates History*, open *Control Panel→All Control Panel Items* (this steps might not be necessary) →*Windows Updates*→Click on *View update history* from left navigation panel→ Click *OK* to close the window.

WINDOWS UPDATES CONFIGURATION

- Open *Change Settings Windows*
- The following options are available to choose to protect system against any known security threads in computing industry.
  - *Install updates automatically (recommended):* System downloads and install *Windows updates* automatically.
  - *Download updates but let me choose whether to install them:* The system downloads *Windows updates* automatically and user chooses the updates that must be installed on a system.
  - *Check for updates but let me choose whether to download and install them:* The system checks updates on regular basis and then user decides which *Windows updates* need to be downloaded and install.
  - *Never check for updates (not recommended):* Microsoft does not recommend this option due to high risk of security threads in computing industry.
  - *Recommended updates:* Only recommended Microsoft updates will be downloaded and installed on a system if this option is enabled.
  - *Who can install updates:* If this option is selected, all local users have permission to install updates on this machine.

OPEN WINDOWS FIREWALL

To configure *Windows Firewall*, open *Windows Firewall* applet by going to *All Control Panel Items*.

WINDOWS FIREWALL CONFIGURATION

It is recommended to configure *Windows Firewall* properly to block unauthorized user access into a system. A hacker may install malicious programs to delete, remove, and modify system registry to make a user system unstable.

To adjust *Windows Firewall* settings, open *Windows Firewall* applet by going to *All*

Control Panel Items. Click on **Turn Windows Firewall on or off** link from left navigation panel to choose one of the following **Windows Firewall** options to configure **Windows Firewall**.

- **Turn on Windows Firewall:** This option is recommended to enable as it protects system against malicious codes that can be installed by a third-party.

- **Block all Incoming Connections:** This option is recommended if user connects to an unsecured connection. An unsecured connection is available for free of charge at the airport or in the coffee shop. All incoming connections will be ignored.

- **Turn off Windows Firewall (not recommended):** This option is not recommended.

By default, **Windows Firewall** is *ON* to protect system integrity. If user would like to disable **Windows Firewall**, choose **Turn off Windows Firewall (not recommended)** option. Click on *Apply* and then click *OK* to save preferences.

WINDOWS FIREWALL EXCEPTIONS

You, as a system administrator, can create a program exception and/or a network port exception to permit users to gain access to a machine or a program. To add a program in the exception list, open **Windows Firewall** applet. From **Windows Firewall** window, click **Allow a program or feature through Windows Firewall** link from left navigation panel. Select a program to allow communication through **Windows Firewall** by selecting the box next to the application. To allow another program through **Windows Firewall**, click on **Allow another program** button to select a program that needs to be added to **Windows Firewall** exception list. Click on *Apply* and then click *OK* to save changes.

MEMORY DIAGNOSTICS TOOL

Memory diagnostics tool checks memory errors. An administrator or a member of an administrative group has privileges to view and create a real-time memory monitoring report.

MEMORY DIAGNOSTICS SCAN

To open *Memory Diagnostics Tool* program:

- Open *All Control Panel Items*
- Open *Administrative Tools*
- Double-click *Memory Diagnostics Tool*

User will be asked to *Restart now and check for problems (recommended)* or *Check for problems the next time I strat my computer* to perform a memory test. Choose one of the above mentioned options and then click on *Close*. Memory test may take few minutes to few hours to perform necessary tests to analyze system memory errors.

PERSONAL COMPUTER BACKUP

A *Personal Computer Backup* is a duplicate copy of user's personal data (e.g., documents and pictures), programs (e.g., Microsoft office), and system registry (which keeps track of hardware and software profile changes). A *PC* restore is a quick way to restore all previously saved user's files, folders, programs, and hardware & software registry configurations in case an operating system crashes. It is recommended to perform a complete *PC* backup at-least once in a week for home users to minimize the risk of losing important data if system fails. In corporate world, system administrators make backups on daily basis.

BACKUP FILES

On corporate level, it is recommended to perform backups on user's files and folders on daily basis. For home users, it is recommended to have a complete backup of their personal files and folders at-least once in a week to minimize the risk of losing personal data over a period of time.

To backup user's files and folders, open *All Control Panel Items*. From *Control Panel* window, open *Backup and Restore*. If system has not configured to backup or restore user's files, click on *Set up backup* link.

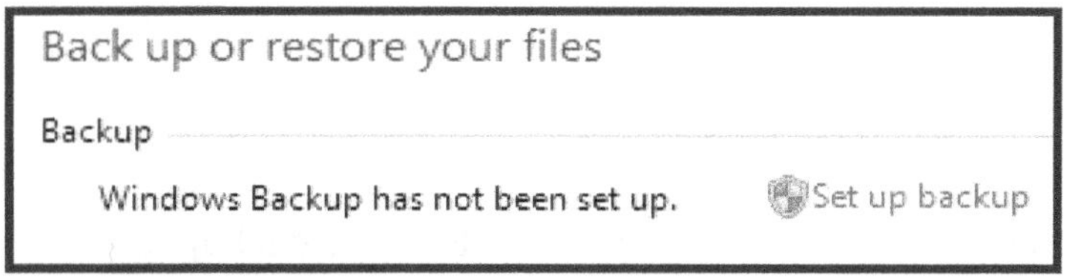

Back up or restore your files

Backup

Windows Backup has not been set up.   Set up backup

Image 2.12: Set up Backup

User will be asked to save personal data in an external device (e.g., CD, DVD, USB drive or any other removable device) or on a network location. To save files in an external hard-drive, connect an external hard-drive with a system to save backup files on it. Choose an appropriate and preferable location to save backup files and then click *Next*.

User will be asked to choose one of the following backup options. It is preferable to choose first option (*Let Windows choose (recommended)*) to save backup files which includes data files from libraries, items from the desktop and default Windows folders.

If user decides to choose first option, Windows will backup necessary system files and folders. By default, system is schedule to backup user's personal data files and folders on every *Sunday* at 7:00 PM. Backup schedule settings can be changed by clicking on *Change Schedule* link. To change backup preferences, adjust following settings and then click on *OK*.

> a. *How often:* Select a Daily, Weekly, or Monthly backup option
>
> b. *What day:* Select an appropriate day of a week
>
> c. *What time:* Select an appropriate time

To run the backup, click on *Save settings and run backup* after reviewing backup settings.

Advanced Windows user may choose second option, *Let me choose.* If user decides to choose second option, user will be asked to decide which folders need to be saved.

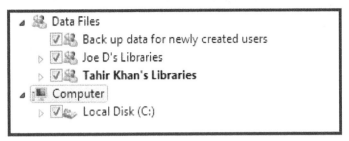

Image 2.13: Choose Backup Files

Click on *Next* after selecting appropriate folders that must include in the backup.

This process may take few minutes to several hours to complete this backup process. If system was successful to backup user's personal files and folders, user will be notified. Click on *Close* to complete this process.

CHANGE BACKUP SETTINGS

Backup location is modifiable anytime. To change a backup location, open ***Backup and Restore*** center. Click on ***Change settings*** link to set a new backup location from ***Backup*** section.

Image 2.14: Set Backup Location

RESTORE FILES

Restore files are the previously backup copies of user's files and folders. To restore user's files and folders, user is required to perform following steps.

- Open **Backup and Restore Center**. In the **Backup and Restore Center** panel, under the **Restore** section, click on **Select another backup to restore files from** link to restore files from an external drive.

- If an individual file or a folder needs to be searched, click on **Restore all users' files** link to search for a file or a folder that needs to be restored.

- Select a preferable backup location and then click on **Next**. If desired backup location is not listed, connect the external drive which holds computer backup copies and then click on **Refresh** button.

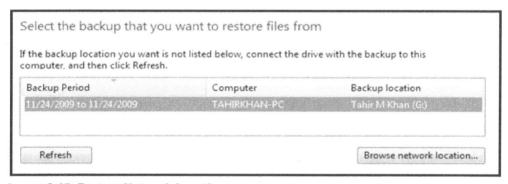

Image 2.15: Browse Network Location

- An individual file or a folder can be browsed by clicking on **Search button.** Type a file name or a folder name in the search bar that needs to be searched. If any desired contents found, select those files and folders to restore and then click on **Next**.

- If all files need to be restored, choose this option, **Select all files from this backup**, to restore system to previous state. Click on **Next**.

- It is recommended to choose default option, **In the original locations**, to restore user's files. Alternately, location of the stored files and folders can be specified by choosing *In the following location* option. To start restoring files, click on *Restore*.

- This restore process may take few minutes to several hours to complete this task depending on the computer speed and performance. Click on *Finish* to complete this process.

- If user prompted for a NTFS (file system) error, user must format the external drive with NTFS file system. To format a drive with NTFS files system, right-click on the drive to select *Format* option from the list. From drop down menu of the *files System*, choose *NTFS* option and then click on *Start* button to format the drive.

INSTALL LOCAL AND NETWORK PRINTERS

To install a local or a network printer:

- Open *Hardware and Sound* applet. Navigate to *Devices and Printers* icon and then click on *Add a printer* link.

- If printer is directly connected with a system, user may install a local printer.

- A local printer can be configured with IP address, subnet mask, and default gateway. Click on *Add a local printer* option to create a new port for a local printer, if needed.

- If a wireless or a Bluetooth printer is available, select *add a network*, *wireless or Bluetooth printer* option to install a network printer.

- An existing port can be used to install a local printer or a network printer. Most common existing ports are *LPT* (*Line Print Terminal*) and *COM* (*Serial Port*). The designated printer's ports such as *LPT*, *COM*, and *USB* (*Universal Serial Bus*) can be used to install a local printer by choosing *Use an existing port* option. If a standard *TCP/IP* port needs to be created, click on *Create a new port* and then select the *Standard TCP/IP port* from drop down menu list. Click on *Next* to continue this process.

- Select **TCP/IP device** from **Device type** category and then type-in printer IP address. If user unaware of the printer IP address, user may consult a network administrator. Click on **Next** to continue installing the printer device.

- This process may take few minutes to install printer drivers. The device drivers must be installed manually if system was unable to detect the printer name and device drivers. To download a printer driver from the manufacture website (user must go to the manufacture website to download latest device drivers, e.g., if user has an HP printer, user must go to www.support.hp.com to download the HP printer drivers) which is faster and reliable method to get the latest printer drivers. If system was successful to detect printer name and device drivers then click on **Next** to continue.

- If system did not detect printer device automatically, additional information needs to be provided to continue installing printer. Select a **Generic Network Card** type which establishes communication between this computer and the network. Check with network administrator to get printer configuration, if needed. Click on **Next**.

- Choose the manufacture name and a printer name and then click on **Next** to download printer device driver. The device driver needs to be installed manually if system did not locate the manufacture name and the printer name.

- To install a printer driver manually, click on **Have Disk**. Navigate to that folder in which device driver are saved and then click on **OK** to start installing the device drivers.

- Click on **Next** to continue installing printer. This process may take several minutes.

- User might be asked to share this printer with other network users. If user would like to share this printer with other network users, type the location of the printer and then click on **Next** otherwise click on **Do not share this printer** option.

- After successful installation of a printer driver, click on **Print a test page.** If test page printed successfully, click on **Finish** to complete the printer installation process.

REMOVE A PRINTER

Open *Hardware and Sound* applet. Navigate to *Devices and Printers* icon to open it. Select a printer device that must be removed and then click on *Remove Device* option from the command bar. If user prompted to confirm this action, click on *Yes* to continue.

Add a device   Add a printer   See what's printing   Print server properties   Remove device

Image 2.16: Printer Command Bar

CONFIGURE PRINTER PORTS

To configure a printer port, open *Hardware and Sound* applet and navigate to *Devices and Printers* icon to open it. To configure a printer port, click the printer which needs to be reconfigured and then select *Print server properties* option from the command bar. In the *Ports* tab, click on *Configure Port* option to modify printer ports settings. Ports can be add, deleted, and reconfigured by clicking on *Add Port*, *Delete Port*, and *Configure Port*, respectively.

To configure printer port settings, type a *Port Name*, a *Printer Name*, or an *IP Address* and then adjust *Raw*, *LPR*, and *SNMP* settings. After making any changes to the printer settings, click *OK* to save preferences.

LIMIT PRINTING TIME

Open *Devices and Printers* window. To enable printing restrictions, choose *Printer Properties* option by right-clicking the printer which needs to be restricted for printing. From *Printer Properties* window, click *Advanced* tab and then select the *Available from* option to adjust the printing time table. By default, printer is always available to print but you, as an administrator, can limit user's privileges by adjusting printing hours, if necessary.

PERMISSION TO MAINTAIN PRINTERS

From *Printer Properties* window, click *Security* tab. User that needs privileges to maintain printer resources can be added to the group to manage following printer resources.

- *Print*: By default, most users have permission to print.

- *Manage printer*: Only local administrator or system administrators can manage printers.

- *Manage documents*: By default, a system administrator has privileges to manage documents.

- *Special permission*: If user needs special permissions, click on *Advanced* button from the *Security* tab to make necessary changes. Only a system administrator is authorized to make such changes to a user profile.

Click on *Apply* to save security settings and then click on *OK* to close the window.

DESKTOP GADGETS

A gadget is a stand-alone program which quickly manages and monitors computer resources, if it is configured properly. For example, a gadget may display a CPU usage meter, multiple clocks, calendars, notes, weather reports, picture slide shows, etc on right side of a computer desktop.

OPEN/ADD/REMOVE DESKTOP GADGETS

To open a gadget:

- Open *All control Panel Items*
- Click on *Desktop Gadget*
- Double-click the gadget that needs to be added to the *Windows Sidebar* from *Sidebar Gadgets* window. To view and download available online gadgets, click *Get more gadgets online* link to add more gadgets to *Windows Sidebar*.
- A gadget from the desktop can be removed by clicking on X (close button)

POWER MANAGEMENT

Power management tool manages power plans to optimize system performance. There are three preferred power plans available which named as: *Balanced*, *Power Saver*, and *High Performance*.

OPEN POWER MANAGEMENT OPTIONS

From *Control Panel* window, open *System and Security*. From *System and Security* window, navigate to *Power Options* link to open it.

Windows 7 provides three power saving plans to optimize system performance.

- *Balanced*: Balanced energy savings and performance
- *Power Saver*: Better energy savings over performance
- *High Performance*: Better performance over energy savings

POWER PLAN SETTINGS

Open *Power Options* from the *Control Panel*. From *Power Options* window, select a preferable power saving plan and then click on *Change Plan Settings* to adjust power plan settings.

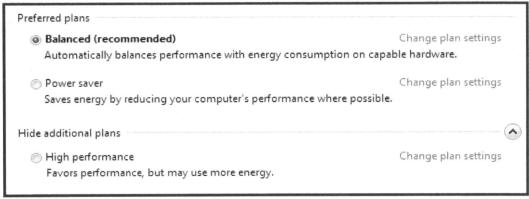

Image 2.17: Preferred Power Plans

From *Edit plan setting* window, adjust *computer display settings* and *computer sleep settings* and then click on *Save Changes*.

CREATE A POWER PLAN

To customize a power plan, click on *Create a Power Plan* link from left navigation pane of the *Power Options* and then type the power plan name. Click on *Create* after adjusting the sleep and display time settings.

REMOVE A POWER PLAN

To remove a customized power plan, click on *Change plan settings* link from *My Custom Plan* section and then click on *Delete this plan* to delete customized power plan. Click on *OK* to delete customized power plan. Only *Customized Power Plans* are modifiable. A user cannot delete *balanced*, *power saver*, and *high performance* power plans.

DEFINE A POWER BUTTON

The function of the power button can be either set to hibernation mode, sleep mode, or do nothing mode by choosing an appropriate power button option. By default, pushing the power button will result in shutting down a computer.

To customize a power button, open *All Control Panel Items* to navigate to the *Power Options* icon to open it. Click *Choose what the power button does* link from left panel of the *Power Options* window.

User can adjust *Power* button settings by selecting a preferable option from drop down menu from the *Power button settings* section. User may set power button function to a *shutdown* mode, a *sleep* mode, a *hibernate* mode, or *do nothing* mode. Click on *Save Changes* after making any changes to the power button.

SYSTEM WAKEUP PASSWORD

Open *Power Options*. Click on *Require a password on wakeup* link from left pane of *Power Options* window.

If *required a password (recommended)* option is grayed out (not available to choose) from *Password protection on wakeup* section, click on *Change settings that are currently unavailable* to change the password protection settings.

It is recommended to have a *wakeup password* to unlock a user computer session. Choose a password protection option and then click on *Save Changes*.

REAL-TIME MONITORING REPORT

Real-time monitoring report collects important information to analyze a computer baseline. A baseline is a snapshot of a system that determines the performance of a computer at any given period of time. It helps to determine bottlenecks [weakest part of a computer component] that slows down the computer performance. To start a system diagnostics report, click *Start* button to type *perfmon /report* [have a space between perfmon and back slash] in the search bar and then hit *Enter* key from a keyboard to run a real-time monitoring report.

Image 2.18: Perfmon /report

Reliability and performance monitor takes about 60 seconds to collect important information about user's local hardware resources, system response time, and application processes. System will generate a diagnostic report with an explanation of diagnostic results. Review results carefully to take necessary action(s) to fix any issue(s), if necessary.

PARENTAL CONTROLS

In past, parents used to buy a third-party software to monitor computer activities. Now, *Parental Controls* is a part of Windows 7 to monitor, restrict, and permit users to not run certain programs, to not surf inappropriate web sites, and to not play inappropiate games. The *Parental Controls* feature is available in all versions of Windows 7. *Parental Control feature* is only applicable to standard user accounts.

OPEN PARENTAL CONTROLS

To open *Parental Controls* program:

- Open *All Control Panel Items*
- Double-click *Parental Controls*

Quick Search

Type *Parental Controls* in search bar

PARENTAL CONTROLS CONFIGURATIONS

Parental controls feature is only applicable to standard user account's activities, not administrator account's activities. Open a standard user account which supposed to be monitored. By default, parental controls feature is turned off. To enforce parental controls, select this option, *On, enforce current settings*, from the *Parental Controls* section. Once the *Parental Controls* is activated for standard users, some or all of the following policies can be enforced.

- *Time limits policy*
- *Control games by rating and content types*
- *Allow and block specific programs per user need, and*
- *View the activity reports to monitor standard user accounts*

ENFORCE TIME LIMITS

To enforce time limits on a standard user account, click the *Time limits* link from *Windows Settings* section. To activate time restrictions policy for standard users, click and drag the hours you, as an administrator, want to block. Click *OK* to save preferences.

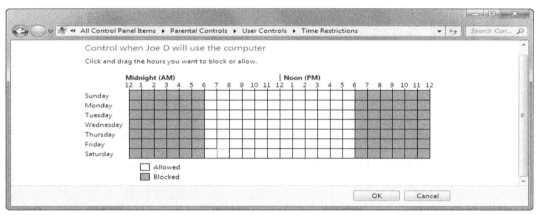

Image 2.19: Time Restrictions

To enforce the game policy on a standard user account, click the *Games* link from *Windows Settings* section. By default, *Windows 7* permits standard users to play all games.

ALLOW OR BLOCK GAMES BY CONTENT TYPES

If you, as an administrator, would like to set game ratings for a standard user, click the *Set game ratings* link from *Block (or allow) games by rating and content types* section and then choose one of the available ratings defined by *Entertainment Software Rating Board*. The ratings are self explanatory. The system administrator has ability to restrict user permission by the game's content type e.g., use of tobacco, sexual violence, etc.

ALLOW OR BLOCK GAMES

To block or allow games, click *Block or Allow specific games* link from *Windows Settings* section. Three options (*user rating setting, always allow,* and *always block*) are available to restrict a standard user to allow or block playing games. Click **OK** to save preferences.

ALLOW OR BLOCK PROGRAMS

To restrict user permission, click **Allow and block specific programs** link from **Windows Settings** section and then choose one of the following options.

- *Windows 7 user can use all programs* (By default, this option is set for standard users)
- *Windows 7 user can only use the programs I allow* (Check appropriate programs that can be used by a user and then click *OK* to save changes)

WINDOWS DEFENDER

Windows 7 machines are pre-loaded with a spyware program, *Windows Defender*, to protect user profile against spywares. It does not provide any protection against viruses. It is a free program for Microsoft users. It is available to download from Microsoft website at http://www.microsoft.com/downloads/details.aspx?FamilyId=435BFCE7-DA2B-4A6A-AFA 4-F7F14E605A0D&displaylang=en&mg_id=10134 (a live link at the time of writing this book). If above mentioned linked is hard to copy into a browser, go to www.google.com and type *Microsoft Windows Defender Downlaod* keywords in the search bar to get a downloadable link to download *Windows Defender* program.

OPEN WINDOWS DEFENDER PROGRAM

To open *Windows Defender* program:

- Open *Control Panel*

- Open *All Control Panel Items*

- Click on *Windows Denfender* icon to start the program

The *Windows Defender* program performs following operations.

- Checks latest Microsoft *Windows Defender* updates

- Quick system scan, full system scan, and customize system scan

- Join Microsoft SpyNet community

- Provides real-time spyware protection

- Manages start-up programs, currently running programs, and winsock services

Image 2.20: Windows Defender Command Bar

WINDOWS DEFENDER UPDATES

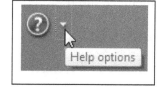

From *Windows Defender* window:

- Click *Help options* (see right margin)

- Select *Check for Updates* option

- If updates are available, process may take few minutes downloading latest spyware definitions. The spyware program provides protection against malicious code that can be installed by a third-party.

WINDOWS DEFENDER - SYSTEM SCANNING OPTIONS

From *Windows Defender* window, click the downward arrow next to the *Scan* tab to choose one of the available options (*Quick Scan*, *Full Scan*, and *Custom Scan*) to scan a system. This process may take several minutes to complete scanning against malicious code, spywares, and unwanted software.

JOIN MICROSOFT SPYNET COMMUNITY

It is recommended to join *Microsoft SpyNet Community* to help identifying and stopping spyware infections:

- Click on *Tools* tab
- Click *Microsoft SpyNet* from the *Settings* section

Microsoft SpyNet is an online community that helps users to choose how to respond to a potential spyware thread. Microsoft recommends users to either subscribe to a basic membership or to an advanced membership; both memberships are free of cost to join. The only difference between both memberships is the amount of information passes to Microsoft. A basic membership sends minimum information associated with a thread. On other hand, an advanced membership sends information which may include location of the software, file name, etc.

Microsoft SpyNet community membership can be unsubscribed at any time by selecting *I don't want to join Microsoft SpyNet at this time* option from bottom of the window. To save membership preferences, click on *Save*.

WINDOWS DEFENDER OPTIONS

From *Windows Defender* window:

- Click on *Tools* tab
- Click *Options* from the *Settings* section

Windows Defender options are divided into following sub-sections:

- *Automatic Scanning - Allow a user to adjust automatically scanning settings*
- *Default Actions - Spyware alert level can be adjusted to high, medium, and low level*
- *Real-time Protection Options - Which programand files needs to be monitor?*
- *Excluded files and folders - Specify files and folders locations that should not be scanned*

- *Excluded file types* - *Specify files types that should not be scanned*

- *Advanced Options* - *Users are capable to scan archieve files, e-mails, and removeable drives. A user can also enable heuristicsoption to detect unwanted software by matching an existing definition of the spyware. It is recommended to create a restore point to revert changes back to default settings in case system craches. If restore point is created before applying actions to the detected items, the system settings will be reverted.*

- *Administrator Options* – The administrator options are:

  - *Use This Program*: By default, this option is set for **Windows Defender**.

  - *Display items from all users of this computer*: By default, administrators have permission to review all **Windows Defender** activities to monitor user's machine against malicious codes and unwanted software.

Make sure to **Save** settings after making any changes to **Windows Defender**.

SNIPPING TOOL

The snipping tool captures snap-shots of a user computer's applications. This tool is available for all Windows 7 editions except **Windows 7 Starter** and **Home Basic** editions. The snipping tool supports HTML, PNG, GIF, and JPEG formats.

To open the *snipping tool*, click *Start* button, click *All Programs*, click *Accessories* and then click **Snipping Tool**. Click the arrow ▼ next to *New* tab to choose one of the following snipping options to capture a screenshot.

  a. *Free-form Snip*

  b. *Rectangular Snip*

  c. *Window Snip*

  d. *Full screen Snip*

EASE OF ACCESS CENTER

The *Ease of Access Center* adjusts accessibility settings. User adjusts on-screen text fonts and also adjusts other program settings which reads the text louder as user moves his mouse cursor or any other pointing device across the desktop. On-screen keyboard is an alternative way to input text using a pointing device or a mouse.

OPEN EASE OF ACCESS CENTER

Open *Control Panel* to navigate to the *Ease of Access* icon to open it. To quickly access *Ease of Access Center* window, press (**Windows key + U)** simultaneously.

WINDOWS MAGNIFIER

From *Ease of Access Center* window, click on *Start Magnifier* to make on-screen text font appear bigger as needed.

WINDOWS 7 NARRATOR CONFIGURATION

From *Ease of Access Center* window, click on *Start Narrator* to modify narrator preferences. Narrator reads the active window content as soon as it starts. To stop *Microsoft Narrator*, click on *Exit* from *Microsoft Narrator* window.

WINDOWS 7 ON-SCREEN KEYBOARD CONFIGURATION

From *Ease of Access Center* window, click on *Start On-Screen Keyboard* to adjust on-screen keyboard settings. *On-Screen Keyboard* inputs the text using the mouse or any other pointing devices.

WINDOWS AERO

Windows Aero is a translucent glass interface for Windows 7 users. *Windows Aero* hardware requirements are following.

- *Windows Display Driver Model* (WDDM) - video card driver
- Directx 9 capable graphics card
- Hardware pixel shader 2.0
- 32-bit per pixel memory and minimum of 128 MB graphics memory

To open *Windows Aero* properties:

- Open *Control Panel*

- Open *Appearance and Personalization*

- From the *Personalization* section, open *Change window glass colors* link

Image 2.21: Personalization

If system supports *Windows Aero*, the *Windows Color and Appearance* window will be prompted to change color scheme of a computer window, *Start Menu* and *Taskbar Menu*. If system does not support *Windows Aero* feature, user will be prompted to *Appearance Settings* dialog box to choose an appropriate color scheme to adjust display settings.

AUTOPLAY DEVICE SETTINGS

AutoPlay settings are default user's system settings to allow an application or a program to open its files with a default interface every time user connects a device to a system.

ADJUST AUTOPLAY DEVICE SETTINGS

To adjust *AutoPlay* device settings, open *Hardware and Sound* applet and then click on *Change default settings for media or devices* link.

Image 2.22: AutoPlay

Default option for a media or a device can be set by selecting a preferable option from drop down menu. If *AutoPlay* settings need to be changed to default settings, click on *Rest all defaults* button (located at button of the window). To save preferences of a device/media, click on *Save*.

CLOCK, LANGUAGE, AND REGION SETTINGS CONFIGURATION

To adjust clock, language, and region settings, perform following steps.

- Open *Control Panel* template. Navigate to *Clock*, *Language*, *and Region* icon to open it to adjust clock, language, and regional settings.

- Click *Regional and Language* options applet from right-panel of the *Clock, Language, and Region* window.

- In the *Format* tab, choose the display format from the *Current format* drop down menu to adjust number, currency, and time & date formats. To customize the format settings, click on *Additional Settings* button to set value for each tab. Click on *Apply* and then click *OK* to save changes.

- In the *Location* tab of the *Regional and language* dialog box, adjust the location of the current system as needed and then click on *Apply* to save changes.

- In *Keyboard and Languages* tab, click on *Change keyboards* button to change a keyboard input language.

- From *Text Services and Input Languages* dialog box, click on *Add* button to install *another* input keyboard language, if needed.

- From *Add Input language* dialog box, click the plus sign next to the language that user wish to install on a system. Select a language and a region in which the user lives in and then click on *OK* to add an alternative input language.

- Now, a new language input pack is available for user to compose e-mails or create documents as needed. Click on *Apply* and then click on *OK* to save changes.

- To remove a language, select the input language that user desires to remove from the *Text Services and Input Languages* window and then click on *Remove*.

TIME AND DATE SETTINGS

To adjust *time and date* settings:

- Open **Control Panel Home**. Navigate to **Clock, Language, and Region** icon to open **Date and Time** applet.

- To modify date and time settings, click **Date and Time** tab and then click on **Change date and time** button.

- To adjust clock time, double-click either hours or minutes or seconds and then use up or down arrows (in front of the clock) to increase or decrease the value. To set the user computer date, use the arrows ▸ ◂ to increase or decrease the months and then click on today's date from the **Date** section. Click on **OK** to save date and time preferences.

DAYLIGHT SAVING TIME CONFIGURATION

To change daylight saving time of a machine, open **Date and Time** applet. In the **Date and Time** tab, click on **Change time zone** button from the **Time zone** section. It is recommended to change the time zone settings as user system moves to a different time zone location. For example, if user moves from Minnesota (a state of United States of America) to California (a state of United States of America) computer time zone must be changed. To enable daylight saving time, check the **Automatically adjust clock for Daylight Saving Time** option. Choose the time zone from the **Time zone** drop down menu and then click on **OK** to save time zone preferences.

INTERNET TIME SERVER SYNCHRONIZATION

To synchronize a machine time with an Internet server time, open **Date and Time** window. From **Date and Time** window, click **Internet Time** tab and then click on **Change settings** button. Select an Internet time server (available Internet time servers are: **time.windows.com, time.nist.gov, time-nw.nist.gov, time-a.nist.gov,** and **time-b.nist.gov**) from **Server** drop down menu and then click on **Update now** button to synchronize this computer clock with the server time. Click **OK** to save changes.

ADDITIONAL CLOCKS CONFIGURATION

To add multiple clocks on a user machine, right-click on the clock (located at right-bottom of the computer desktop) and then choose *Adjust Date/Time* option. From *Date and Time* dialog box, click *Additional Clocks* tab to select this option, *Show this clock*. Select clock time zone and then enter an appropriate display name for each clock. User can add additional two clocks excluding the system clock on a system. Click on *Apply* and then click *OK* to save settings. To view additional clocks, move the mouse cursor over the system clock.

DEVICE MANAGER

Device Manager provides an overview of installed hardware devices of a computer. A hardware device will not run properly unless device drivers are installed and configured properly. Only system administrators or a member of an administrator group has privileges to make changes to the *Device Manager*.

OPEN DEVICE MANAGER

To open *Device Manager*:

- Open *All Control Panel Items*
- Double-click *Device Manager*

ENABLE HARDWARE DEVICE

From *Device Manager* window, expand the device section by clicking on an arrow sign next to it. If a device is disabled, a downward arrow with a circle around it will appear on that device. To enable a device, choose *Enable* option by right-clicking on the device component.

Image 2.23: Network Adapters - Disabled Device

DISABLE HARDWARE DEVICE

From *Device Manager* window, expand the device section by clicking on an arrow sign next to it. A hardware device can be disabled by right-clicking on the device component and then by choosing the *Disable* option from the list. It is not recommended to disable any hardware devices unless it is required.

WAKEUP NETWORK ADAPTOR

Open *Device Manager*. Click on the arrow sign next to the *Network adapters* to expand the device components. Choose *Properties* option by right-clicking on the device component which listed under the *Network adapters*.

Image 2.24: Network Adaptor - Wakeup Device

From *Network Adaptor Properties* window, click *Power Management* tab and then check the *Allow this device to wake the computer* option to allow system administrators to wake up user system remotely to perform scheduled maintenance whenever it is necessary. Click on *OK* to save changes. It is not recommended to enable this feature unless it is necessary.

UPDATE DEVICE DRIVER

Windows 7 operating system is capable of searching latest device drivers automatically. User must be connected with the Internet to download latest device drivers automatically. If *Windows 7* is unable to download latest drivers automatically, then user is required to download device drivers manually from the manufacture website.

A yellow circle around the device icon shows no sign of communication between this device and other devices of a system.

Image 2.25: Other Devices

To establish a connection between this device and other devices of a system, the device driver must be installed. To update a device driver, right-click on the yellow circled device to select the *Update Driver Software* option from the list.

To allow a system to download and install a device driver automatically, choose *Search automatically for updated driver software* option. Windows may take several minutes to search for a device driver. If Windows was successful to download and install the device driver, user will be notified. Re-boot the machine to apply changes to a system.

To manually install a device driver, choose *Browse my computer for driver software* option. User must download the device driver from the manufacture website, for example, if user has a dell machine, user must go to www.support.dell.com to download latest device driver. Save the device driver into a local computer hard-drive. After downloading device driver, navigate to the folder in which the device driver is saved and then click on *Next*. Windows may take several minutes installing the device driver. User will be notified, if device drivers are found and installed correctly.

ROLLING BACK DEVICE DRIVER

To roll back a device driver, open *Device Manger*. From *Device Manager* window, expand the device by clicking the arrow sign next to it. Choose *Properties* option by right-clicking on that device.

From *Device Properties* window, click *Driver* tab and then click on *Roll Back Driver* button to roll the device driver back to the previous stage. This process may re-boot user system to complete this process.

START MENU

Windows Start Menu is a user interface to view and launch programs (e.g., *Microsoft Office* products, *Control Panel*, *Administrative Tools*, *Network utilities*, etc) that are currently installed on a user system. Microsoft users may search programs and files by typing-in keywords in search field located at left-bottom of the *Start Menu*.

Start Menu can be accessed by clicking on *Start button* (located at left-bottom of the desktop) or pressing *Windows Logo Key* from a keyboard.

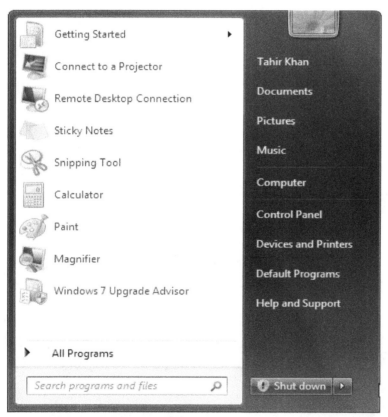

Image 2.26: Start Menu Interface

START MENU CUSTOMIZATION

Choose *Properties* option by right-clicking on *Start* button. Click on *Customize* button from *Taskbar and Start Menu Properties* window to customize *Start Menu* folders, favorites, and programs.

Select appropriate preferences to customize **Start Menu** links and icons from the *Customize Start Menu* dialog box. Click *OK* to save changes.

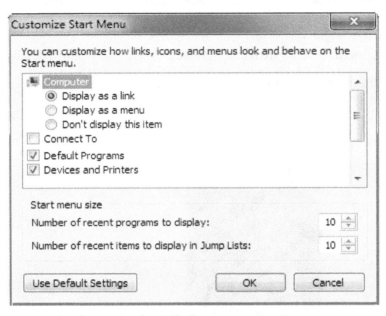

Image 2.27: Customize Start Menu

The following privacy options can be adjusted to:

- *Store and display recently opened programs in the Start menu*

- *Store and display recently opened items in the Start menu and the taskbar*

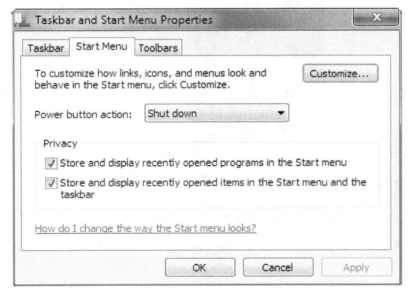

Image 2.28: Taskbar and Start Menu Properties

TASK MANAGER

System administrators use ***Windows Task Manager*** to manage currently running applications, processes, and system services. To quickly access ***Task Manager*** window, press ***Ctrl, Shift, and Esc*** keys simultaneously.

Open ***Windows Task Manager*** by right-clicking on the ***Taskbar*** (by default, located at bottom of the desktop) and then by choosing the ***Start Task Manager*** option from the list. A ***Task Manager*** performs following operations.

- *Manages applications that are currently running in the system.*

- *Manages/monitor processes that CPU and memory is performing.*

- *Manages application Services that are currently running on this computer.*

- *Monitors CPU and Memory performance of this computer.*

- *Networking (Wireless or Wired networking performance status).*

- *List of the users who are currently logged-on or were logged-on to this machine earlier.*

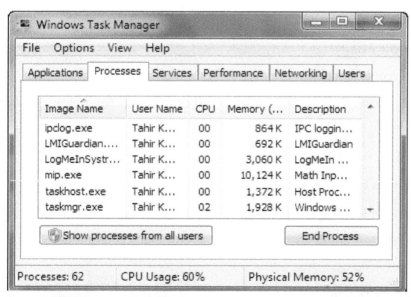

Image 2.29: Windows Task Manager

Windows Task Manager enhances a system administrator's capability to either start or end an application process or their dependencies services. This is not the best tool to monitor networking performance to analyze and troubleshoot issues that a user might have with his system but basic networking monitoring can be done through **Windows Task Manager**.

TASKBAR

Taskbar displays currently running applications. By default, it is located at bottom of the Microsoft Windows operating system. To move the taskbar right, left, bottom, or top of the screen, just drag it to a preferable location. The taskbar is dragable as long as it is not locked. To unlock the taskbar, right-click on the task to clear **Lock the taskbar** option.

Image 2.30: Taskbar Interface

TASKBAR PROPERTIES

Right click on the taskbar to choose **Properties** option from the list. From **Taskbar and Start Menu Properties** window, click **Taskbar** tab to adjust some or all of the available preferences.

- *Lock the taskbar*
- *Auto-hide the taskbar*
- *Use small icons*
- *Taskbar location on screen – Choose either Bottom, Top, Right, or Left option*
- *Taskbar buttons – Available options are:*
    i. *Always combine, hide labels*
    ii. *Combine when taskbar is full*
    iii. *Never*
- *Notification Area*
- *Use Desktop Preview*

Click on **Apply** and then click **OK** to save **Taskbar** changes.

EXTERNAL HARD DRIVE ON TASKBAR

Right click on the *Taskbar*, point to the *Toolbars* and then click the *New Toolbar*.

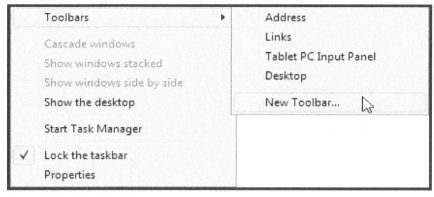

Image 2.31: New Toolbar

Browse to select the external device (e.g., external hard-drive, USB drive, etc) that user would like to add on the taskbar. To access content of an external drive, click the ***double arrow*** (located at top of the drive name).

If user would like to remove an external device from *Taskbar*, right-click on *Taskbar* and then point to the *Toolbars* to remove the *selected Drive* (click on selected drive to remove a device from *Taskbar*).

Image 2.32: External Device on Taskbar

INTERNET EXPLORER BROWSER

Internet Explorer (IE) is part of Windows 7 and it adds an extra layer of security for Windows 7 users to protect their personal data against viruses and spywares.

INTERNET EXPLORER GENERAL OPTIONS

Open *Internet Explorer* browser, go to the *Tools* menu to choose *Internet Options*. Tools menu is located at upper-right corner of the explorer window. If tools menu is not visible on right side of the *Internet Explorer* window, press *Alt* key (from a keyboard) to display tools menu bar on top of the explorer window.

CHANGE INTERNET EXPLORER BROWSER HOMEPAGE

To change *Internet Explorer* homepage, open *Internet Explorer* browser. From *Internet Options* dialog box, click **General** tab, under the *Home page* section, type the *URL* (*Uniform Resource Locator*) of a website to set *Internet Explorer* homepage.

If multiple IE homepages needs to be added, type each website address in a new line in the *Home Page* section. Each website will open its own web browser tab. Click on *Apply* and then click *OK* to save IE settings.

DELETE BROWSING HISTORY

Internet Explorer browser keeps track of temporary Internet files, images, media files, and personal information.

To delete Internet browsing history, open *Internet Options* window. From *Internet Options* window, click *General* tab, under the *Browsing history* section, click on *Delete* button to remove some or all of the browsing history contents. Click on *Yes* to confirm this action to delete *Internet Explorer* browsing history. This process may take few minutes.

CUSTOMIZE BROWSING HISTORY SETTINGS

To adjust browsing history settings, open *Internet Options* window. From *Internet Options* window, click *General* tab, under the *Browsing history* section, click on *Settings* to customize browser settings.

By default, *Internet Explorer* keeps record of visited web pages history for 20 days. User can specify the days in the *History* section by typing the number of days that a user wish to keep pages in history. Click *OK* to save changes. If visited web pages value is set to 0, the browser will never keep websites history, temporary files, and cookies history.

INTERNET EXPLORER PRIVACY OPTIONS

Internet Explorer Privacy options configure pop-up blocker and web browser cookies settings. Generally, a computer cookie saves usernames, passwords, e-mail addresses and other related information that user frequently uses online. Two kinds of cookies are associated with a web page, first-party cookies and third-party cookies. The first-party cookies that come from the website that a user is currently visiting and third-party cookies come from the websites other than the ones user currently surfing but they are associated with the website that a user currently surfing.

INTERNET PRIVACY SETTINGS

To adjust *Internet Privacy* settings, open *Internet Options* window. From *Internet Options* window, click *Privacy* tab, under the *Settings* section, move the slider up and down to change *Internet Zones* settings (*Internet, local intranet, trusted sites*, and *restricted sites*). Choose one of the following options to adjust Internet privacy settings. Click on *Apply* and then click *OK* to save *Internet Explorer* privacy preferences.

- *Block all cookies:* Block all cookies from all websites. This option is not recommended due to the high privacy of blocking all cookies from all websites.

- *High:* Block cookies that save information that can be used to contact user without his/her explicit consent. It also blocks all cookies from websites that do not have a compact privacy policy.

- *Medium High:* Block third-party cookies and first-party cookies to save information that can be used to contact user without his/her explicit and implicit consent, respectively. It also blocks third-party cookies that do not have a compact privacy policy.

- *Medium:* This option blocks third-party cookies that do not have a compact privacy policy. It only restricts first-party cookies to save information that can be used to contact user without his/her implicit knowledge. It also blocks third-party cookies to save information that can be used to contact user without his/her explicit consent. This option is recommended to enable.

- *Low:* This option restricts third-party cookies to save information that can be used to contact user without his/her implicit consent. It also blocks third-party cookies that do not have compact privacy policy.

- *Accept all cookies:* This option allows accepting all cookies from all websites. This option is not recommended as it accepts all cookies from all websites.

PER SITE PRIVACY

To adjust *Per Site Privacy* settings, open *Internet Options* window. From *Internet Options* window, click *Privacy* tab, under the *Settings* section, click on *Sites* to set privacy settings for certain websites that supposed to be always accepting or blocking cookies regardless of their privacy policy.

To manage a website address, type the address of that website in the provided field and then click on *Block* or *Allow* button to add that website to the *Managed websites* category. A blocked website would never get any cookies; on the other hand the allowed websites always get cookies regardless of their privacy policy settings. Click *OK* to save *Per Site Privacy* settings.

REMOVE MANAGED WEBSITES

To remove a site from the list of the managed websites, click *Privacy* tab from *Internet Options* dialog box and then click on *Sites* from the *Settings* section. Select a website to remove from the list of the managed websites and then click on *Remove*. If user would like to remove managed websites list, click on *Remove All*. Click *OK* to exit out of the managed website window.

INTERNET EXPLORER SECURITY OPTIONS

Internet Explorer security options adjust security level zone settings for *Internet*, *local intranet*, *trusted sites*, and *restricted sites*. The user will be restricted to download any materials from these websites which are added to the restricted sites zone list.

PROTECTED MODE

To enable *protected mode*, open *Internet Options* window. From the *Internet Options* window, click *Security* tab, under the *Security level for this zone* section, select the *Enable Protected Mode (requires restarting Internet Explorer)* option to enable *Internet Explorer* protected mode. Click on *Apply* and then click *OK* to save changes.

RESET INTERNET EXPLORER SETTINGS

Internet Explorer settings keep track of the user temporary browser files, browser add-ons and toolbars, visited websites history, and cookies. A cookie saves user's passwords, usernames, Website URLs and other related information that a user frequently uses online.

To reset *Internet Explorer* settings, open *Internet Options* window. From *Internet Options* window, click *Advanced* tab, click on *Reset* button to reset browser default settings from the *Reset Internet Explorer settings* section. Resetting *Internet Explorer* settings do not affect favorite's settings, *web feed contents* settings, *Internet connection* settings, *Group Policy* settings, and *Content Advisor* settings.

The following *Internet Explorer* settings can be reset by clicking on *Reset* button.

- Disable toolbars and add-ons
- Default web browser settings
- Privacy and Security settings
- Advanced options
- Tabbed browsing settings
- Pop-up settings
- Delete personal settings

This process may take several minutes deleting browser history, browser add-ons, and browser settings. Click on *Close* button to close the window.

POP-UP BLOCKER SETTINGS

To adjust pop-up blocker settings, open *Internet Options* window. From *Internet Options* window, click *Privacy* tab, click on *Settings* from the *Pop-up blocker* section.

Type an address of a website in *Address of website to allow* search field and then click on *Add* button to enter that website to allowed sites list. Any website which is added to the *Allowed sites* will accept pop-ups.

To remove a website from allowed sites list, click the website which supposed to be removed and then click on *Remove*. If user desires to remove entire allowed sites list, click on *Remove all*.

If user would like to see a warning message whenever a pop-up is blocked by the browser, check *Show Information Bar when a pop-up is blocked* option from *Notifications and filter level* section to enable this feature. Once this feature is active, an information bar will be displayed on *Internet Explorer* browser to inform user about blocked websites.

If user would like to hear a warning sound whenever a pop-up is blocked for any website, check *Play a sound when a pop-up is blocked* option from the *Notifications and filter level* section to enable this feature. To adjust pop-up filter level setting, choose one of the following options from drop down menu of *Filter Level* to customize pop-up filter level settings.

- *High*: Block all pop-ups
- *Medium*: Block most automatic pop-ups
- *Low*: Allow pop-ups from secure sites

TURN ON POP-UP BLOCKER

To turn on *Pop-up Blocker*:

- Open *Internet Explorer* browser
- Click *Tools* menu
- Click *Pop-up Blocker*
- Click *Turn On Pop-up Blocker*
- Click on *Yes* to confirm this action

It is recommended to keep pop-up blocker turned on while surfing web.

TURN OFF POP-UP BLOCKER

To turn off *Pop-up Blocker*:

- Open *Internet Explorer* browser
- Click *Tools* menu
- Click *Pop-up Blocker*
- Click *Turn Off Pop-up Blocker*
- Click on *Yes* to confirm turning off pop-up blocker settings

CONTENT ADVISOR

Content Advisor blocks objectionable contents of a website. A user may be required to enter supervisor password to view the contents of a restricted website, if it is configured properly.

ICRA3 CONTENT LEVEL RATING

ICRA3 is an *Internet Explorer* browser rating system to allow or block inappropriate web pages. To view the ICRA3 content level rating, open *Internet Options* window. From *Internet Options* window, click *Content* tab, click on *Enable* from *Content Advisor* section. User may need administrative privileges to make any changes to the *Content Advisor* settings.

In the *Ratings* tab, select the rating category of your choice to view the content ratings from the *Select a category to view the rating levels* box. To adjust content ratings, slide the slider left or right from *Adjust the slider to specify what users are allowed to see* section. It is recommended to read rating category contents in the *Description* section before applying any changes to the browser. Click on *Apply* and then click *OK* to save *Content Advisor* preferences.

CONTENT ADVISOR APPROVED WEBSITES

Open *Internet Options* window. From *Internet Options* window, click *Content* tab. From *Content Advisor* section click on *Enable*. In the *Approved Sites* tab, type a website address to either permit or restrict a user to view the website contents regardless of how it is rated. To allow a user to view the content of a website, type the address of that website in the search bar and then click on *Always* button. On the other hand, inappropriate content websites can be added to disapprove sites list. Type the address of a website in the search field and then click on *Never* button to add that website to the disapproved website list.

If a website is approved to view, a green circle with a tick mark will appear in front of it. For disapproved websites, a red circle around a white line will display in front of it. Click on *Apply* and then *OK* to save settings.

If user has not created an administrative password to manage *Content Advisor* feature, user will be prompted to setup an administrative password. Type the password and then click *OK* to save settings.

To remove an approved *Content Advisor* website, select the address of that website that user wishes to remove from the *List of approved and disapproved websites* box and then click on *Remove*. User can only remove one website at a time. Click on *Apply* and then *OK* to save settings.

CHANGE CONTENT ADVISOR SUPERVISOR PASSWORD

Open *Internet Options* window. From *Internet Options* window, click *Content* tab. Click on *Settings* to change *Content Advisor* password from the *Content Advisor* section. Click *General* tab, under the *Supervisor password* section, click on *Change password*.

User must type an old password and then type a new password that user would like to set for *Content Advisor*. Type the password hint, if necessary. Click *OK* to save password.

WEBSITE CONTENTS PERMISSION

Open *Internet Options* window. From *Internet Options* window, click *Content* tab to click on *Settings* from *Content Advisor* section. To allow users to visit no rating website contents, check the *Users can see websites that have no rating* option from the *User options* section of the *General* tab. Click on *Apply* and then click *OK* to save settings.

To allow users to access restricted website contents without requiring a supervisor password. Click *General* tab from the *Content Advisor* window to clear the *Supervisor can type a password to allow users to view restricted content* checkbox from the *User options* section. User will not be asked to enter a supervisor password to view the restricted website contents. Click on *Apply* and then click *OK* to save *Content Advisor* preferences.

AUTO COMPLETE

An *AutoComplete* keeps track of all previous stored entries, e.g., usernames, passwords, and URLs that user has previously entered on a website. To adjust *AutoComplete* settings, open *Internet Options* window. From *Internet Options* window, click *Content* tab. From the *AutoComplete* section click on *Settings*. If user would like to be asked to save password every time user visits a new website, check *Prompt me to save passwords* option from *Use AutoComplete for* section. Check the appropriate options and then click *OK* to save preferences.

FEED CONTENTS

Feed contents are the latest headlines that are frequently published by a website, such as a blog group and contents of a newspaper. If user frequently visits an online newspaper to read latest news, user can subscribe to read only updated contents of the website since your last visit. The feed contents are also known as *Really Simple Syndication* (RSS) feeds, XML feeds, syndicated content, web feeds, or channel.

CONFIGURE FEED CONTENTS SETTINGS

To adjust feed contents settings, open *Internet Options* window. From *Internet Options* window, click *Content* tab. Click on *Settings* from the *Feeds* section.

In the *Feed Settings* dialog box, under the *Default schedule* section, check *Automatically check feeds for updates* option and then select how often *Internet Explorer* must check for feed updates. User has following options to choose from: *15 minutes*, *30 minutes*, *1 hour*, *4 hours*, *1 day*, and *1 week*. Choose an appropriate time frame to check latest feed contents update.

To manage advanced feed contents, select one of the following options.

- *Automatically mark feed as read when reading a feed*

- *Turn on feed reading view*

- *Play a sound when a feed is found for a webpage*

Click *OK* to save feed contents settings.

DOWNLOAD GOOGLE CHROME

Go to the http://www.google.com/chrome website to download a *Google Chrome* browser. Click on the ***Download Google Chrome*** link to read and accept terms and condition of installing and using the browser, if user accepts browser terms and conditions, click on ***Accept and Install*** button.

User will be asked to either run or save the ***Google Chrome*** setup file. Run the setup file to install the browser. It may take few minutes to install the browser. Click on ***Start Google Chrome*** to run the browser.

CHROME OPTIONS

Open ***Chrome*** browser. Click the ***maintenance*** icon (located at far most right top side of the browser) to adjust settings.

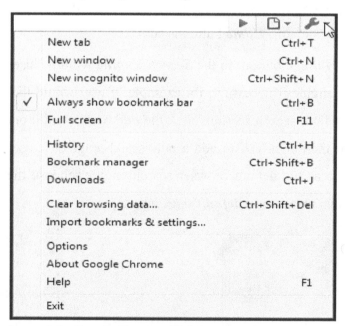

Image 3.1: Google Chrome - Maintenance Menu

To open ***Google Chrome*** options window, click on ***Options*** from the menu bar. Basic Chrome options are divided into four sections named as ***on startup***, ***home page***, ***default search***, and ***default browser***.

In the *On startup* section, user can set *Google Chrome* web page preferences. Google Chrome allows users to open multiple web pages by first clicking on *Open the following pages* option and then by adding desire Web pages in the list. The currently listed pages can be removed from the list by highlighting the Web page link and then by clicking on *Remove* button.

In the *Home page* section, users are allowed to display home page internally or open a new blank tab within the browser. User can set a web home page by typing a website address in front of the *Open this page* option field. Every time user starts *Chrome* browser, user will be directed to the specified home page. If user would like to get a blank home page, click on *Use the New Tab page* option.

The above mentioned preferences are only active if *Home page* button in enabled. Home page section permits users to display *Home* button on the toolbar by checking the *Show Home button on the toolbar* option. By default, *Home* button is active.

To manage search engines, click on *Manage* button. In the *Search Engine* window, user has permission to add a new search engine if necessary, for example, if user would like to add a AOL search engine in the default search section, click the *add* button to fill out *Name*, *keyword*, and *URL* filed and then click *OK* to add a new search engine. If user would like to set *AOL* search engine as his default browser search engine, choose the *AOL* search engine from the drop down menu from *default search* section.

Image 3.2: Add Search Engine

In *Default browser* section, click on *Make Google Chrome my default browser* to make the *Google Chrome* browser as of your default browser.

MINOR TWEAKS

Google Chrome permits users to tweak following options to set user's preferences:

- *Download location link*
- *Passwords settings*
- *Fonts and languages settings*, and
- *Form autofill settings*

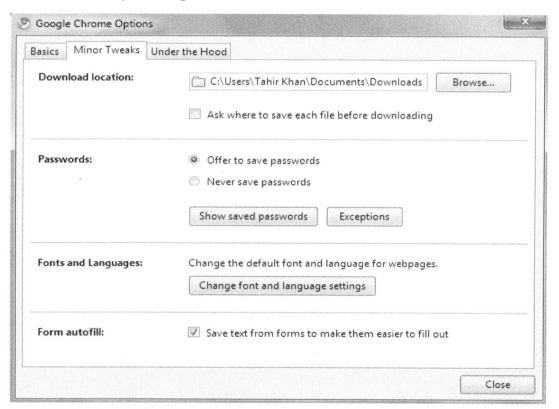

Image 3.3: Google Chrome - Minor Tweaks

In the *Download location* section, user has option to set the download location manually by typing the correct path in the search filed or by specifying the location by clicking on *Browse* button. All downloaded files from Internet will be saved in that folder. By default, all downloaded files are saved into a *Downloads* folder. If a user would like to be asked to specify the location of a file at the time of downloading, select this option *Ask where to save each file before downloading*.

In the *Passwords* section, user has option to either allow browser to save web passwords or never save passwords for any Web page. The browser saved passwords can be viewed by clicking on *Show saved passwords* button.

In *Fonts and Languages* section, user has ability to choose preferable font and language settings by clicking on *Change font and language settings* button.

In *Form autofill* section, by default *Google Chrome* browser enables *Form autofill* option for online users to quickly fill out online forms by using the same information that is being entered previously.

PRIVACY OPTIONS

Privacy options are recommended to be adjusted to improve a web browser performance.

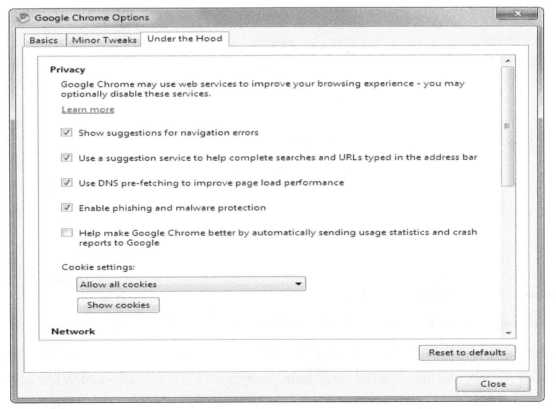

Image 3.4: Google Chrome - Under the Hood

In the ***Privacy*** section, ***Chrome*** users can customize privacy options to adjust and improve browsing experience.

Adjust cookies settings by choosing one of the following available options.

- *Allow all cookies* (Recommended, and enabled by default)
- *Restrict how third-party cookies can be used*
- *Block all cookies*

The cookies list that has been added to the brower can be viewed by clicking on ***Show cookies*** button. If cookies needs to be deleted regardless of any reasons, select the cookies entry that must be removed and then click on ***Remove*** button. If all cookies need to be removed, click on ***Removed*** button. Removing all browser cookies are not recommended.

CLEAR BROWSING DATA

To clear browsing data, click on ***maintenaince*** icon from the far top right side of the brower to choose ***Clear Browsing Data*** option, otherwise press ***Ctrl + Shift + Delete*** button simultaneously.

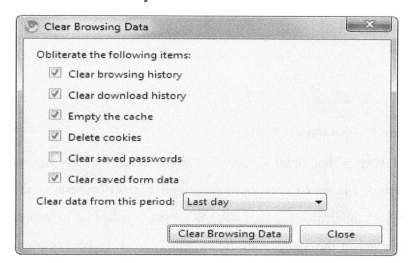

Image 3.5: Google Chrome - Clear Browsing Data

If *Chrome* user would like to clear the browsing data, click on *Clear Browsing Data* button to clear browsing history, clear download history, empty the cache, clear saved passwords, delete cookies, and clear saved form data. Also, the browser has option to delete last day, last week, last 4 weeks cookies, or everything that has been saved since the browser is installed on a user machine by selecting an appropriate option from drop down menu of *Clear data from this period*.

IMPORT BOOKMARKS AND SETTINGS

To import bookmarks from *Microsoft Internet Explorer* or *Firefox* browser, click the *maintenaince* icon from far top right side of the brower and then click on *Import Bookmarks and Settings*.

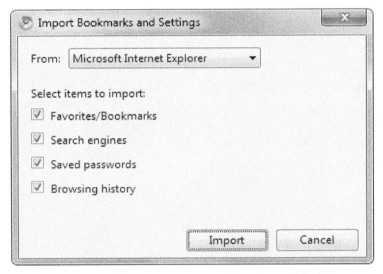

Image 3.6: Google Chrome - Import Bookmarks and Settings

Chrome users may import favorites, bookmarks, search engines, saved passwords, and browsing history from *Microsoft Internet Explorer* browser and *Firefox* browser to the *Google Chrome* browser. Select the browser which you, as a user, would like to import the bookmarks from and then select the appropriate items which needs to be imported. Click on *Import* button to start importing bookmarks to *Chrome* browser. It may take few minutes to import selected items from a desire browser to the *Google Chrome* browser.

USER ACCOUNT CONTROL POLICY

The *Group Policy Object* (GPO) enhances system administrator's capabilities to control hardware and software settings of a user's profile to minimize system security risk. GPO can only be deployed with *Windows 7 Professional*, *Ultimate* and *Enterprise* editions. User must be an administrator or must have administrator privileges to enforce *Local Security Policy*.

OPEN LOCAL SECURITY SETTING EDITOR

To open *Local Security Setting Editor*, run command prompt (*Windows Key + R*) to type *secpol.msc* in the search bar and then click *OK*.

LOCAL SECURITY ACCOUNT POLICY

The local security account policy enforces password history policy, maximum password age policy, minimum password length policy, password complexity requirement policy, and reversible encryption policy.

To open *security account policy*:

- Open *All Control Panel Items*
- Double-click *Administrative Tools*
- Double-click *Local Security Policy*
- From left navigation panel, double-click *Account Policies* folder
- Double-click *Password Policy* folder

To enforce the password policy, user must be a system administrator or must have administrative privileges to make changes to the password policy. The following policies can be enforced for a local user account.

ENFORCE PASSWORD HISTORY

To enforce the password history policy, double-click *Enforce password history* policy and then type a numeric value (choose between 1 and 24) in *Keep password history for* box. To enforce this policy, a numeric number must be greater than 1 and less than 25. Click on *Apply* and then click *OK* to save settings.

MAXIMUM PASSWORD AGE

To enforce the maximum password age policy, double-click *Maximum password age* policy. Maximum password age must be between 1 and 999 days and it should not be less than minimum password age. If the maximum password age is set to 0, then user password will never expire. It is recommended to set user password policy to expire every 30 to 90 days to minimize security risk. Click on *Apply* and then click *OK* to save settings.

To enforce the minimum password age policy, double-click *Minimum password age* policy and then type a numeric value that must be any value between 1 and 998. The minimum password age must be less than maximum password age policy. If the maximum password age is set to 0, then the minimum password can be set to any values between 0 and 998.

MINIMUM PASSWORD LENGTH

To enforce the minimum password length policy, double-click *Minimum password length* policy to type a numeric value that must be between 1 and 14 characters. If minimum password character length is set to 0, then minimum password length policy is not enforced. By default, the minimum password length for the domain controller is 7 characters and 0 for the stand-alone servers.

PASSWORD COMPLEXITY REQUIREMENTS

To activate this policy, double-click *Password must meet complexity requirements* policy and then select *Enabled* option to enforce it. Click on *Apply* and then click *OK* to save password complexity requirement preferences. By default, this policy is enabled on domain controllers and disabled on stand-alone servers.

User must meet following password complexity requirements to setup a secret password.

- User's account name should not be used as a part of the password
- User's password should not have two consecutive characters of user's full name

- The password length must be at-least six characters long
- Should contain at-least one uppercase character (A through Z), at-least one lowercase character (a through z), at-least one digit (0 through 9), or at-least one non-alphabetic character (@, #. $, %, ^, &, *,!, etc)

STORE PASSWORDS USING REVERSIBLE ENCRYPTION

The *Store passwords using reversible encryption* policy keeps track of user's passwords to provide application support which require having knowledge of user's stored passwords. By default, this policy is disabled and it is recommended to have this setting disabled due to security reasons.

To enforce this policy, double-click *Store passwords using reversible encryption* policy and then select *Enabled* option. Click on *Apply* and then click *OK* to save reversible encryption preferences. This policy must be enabled to perform any specific action that requires having the knowledge of stored passwords using reversible encryption.

LOCAL SECURITY ACCOUNT LOCKOUT POLICY

The local security account policy enforces *account lockout duration* policy, *account lockout threshold* policy, and *reset account lockout counter after* policy.

ACCOUNT LOCKOUT THRESHOLD

Open *Local Security Settings Editor*. From left navigation panel, click the *Account Lockout Policy* folder from the *Security* settings section.

From right navigation panel, double-click *Account Lockout Threshold* policy and type any value between 0 and 999 in the *Account will lock out after* box. Click on *Apply* and then click *OK* to save changes.

A locked-out account may only be reset by a system administrator or the user must wait until the lockout duration for that account has expired. If invalid log-on attempts value is set to 0, then a user account will never lockout even after many failed log-on attempts. It is recommended to enable this option to improve system security.

An account lockout threshold policy may affect *Account lockout duration* policy and *Reset account lockout counter after* policy, if user accepts the suggested 30 minutes value for each policy. Click *OK* to save changes.

LOCAL POLICIES

Local policies audit account logon events, account management events, and user's rights of accessing this computer locally or remotely.

AUDIT ACCOUNT LOGIN EVENTS

Open *Local Security Settings Editor*. From left navigation panel, under the *Security* settings section, double-click the *Local Policies* folder and then click on *Audit policy* folder to audit account login events.

Double-click on audit account login events to set a local system policy. Account logon events can be either audited for a success event or a failure event. If a system administrator would like to monitor user success logon events, the *Success* box must be checked otherwise check *Failure* box. Click *OK* to save preferences.

Image 4.1: Audit Account Login Events

A system administrator can audit more events by using the same technique explained above.

USER RIGHTS ASSIGNMENT

Open *Local Security Settings Editor*. From left navigation panel, under the *Security* settings section, double-click the *Local Policies* folder and then click on *User Rights Assignment* folder. From right-hand side window, a system administrator can permit or deny user's rights by double-clicking on a desire policy.

For example, if a system administrator would like to add a user to a group policy that has privileges to access this computer locally, the administrator will double-click on *Allow log on locally* policy to open the desired policy to add a user to this policy. Policy shows the list of users who can access this computer locally if you, as a system administrator, would like to remove a user from the list, click on the user's name and then click on *Remove* button to deny user access to this computer locally or add a user by clicking on *Add User or Group* button.

Image 4.2: Local Security Setting - Allow Log on Locally

All other user's rights assignment policies can be modified by using the same technique.

SECURITY OPTIONS POLICY

Open *Local Security Settings Editor*. From left navigation panel, under the *Security* settings section, double-click *Local Policies* folder and then click on *Security Options* folder. From the right-hand side window, a system administrator can permit or deny user rights by double-clicking on a desire policy.

To activate a security policy, double-click the policy and then select *Enabled* option to enforce a policy. Click on *Apply* and then click *OK* to save preferences. If enabled or disabled options are not available, user may choose an option from drop down menu to set a security policy.

AUDIT A USER

A system administrator can audit a user to keep track of changes that can be made to a file, a document and the system registry of a machine. Auditing a user is the best way to limit user's privileges to improve system security.

To monitor a document changes: right-click on a document that must be audited and then select the *Properties* option from the list.

Click *Security* tab and then click on *Advanced* button to set user permission.

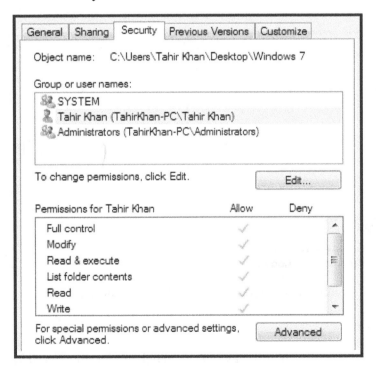

Image 4.3: Security Advanced Settings

Click the *Auditing* tab and then click on *Continue*. User must be an administrator or a member of an administrative group or must have administrative privileges to perform this task.

Add a user by clicking on *Add* button.

Image 4.4: Auditing Entries Window

Enter the name of a user or a group in the ***Enter the object name to select*** box and then click **OK**. Only an active user is auditable. If you, as a system administrator, enter the name of a user who is not an active user, a warning message will be prompted. Click **OK** to save preferences.

VIEW AUDIT LOG

Open ***Administrative Tools*** from the ***Control Panel***. In the ***Administrative tools*** panel, navigate and double-click on ***Event Viewer*** icon to start the program. If user prompted for administrative credentials, provide administrative credentials to continue this process.

In left navigation pane of the ***Event Viewer***, double-click the ***Windows Logs*** folder from the ***Event Viewer (Local)*** section to open ***Security*** option.

Other ***Windows Logs*** (***Application***, ***Setup***, ***System***, and ***Forwarded Events***) are also viewable by clicking on the log entries. The log entries are displayed on right-hand side of the panel. To view a log entry, double-click on the log entry.

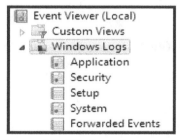

Image 4.5: Windows Logs

In right navigation pane of a *Windows Log*, from the *Security* section, double-click an event to view changes that were made to a document by an audited user. In addition, an audit report includes the log name, source, event id, level, user name (if applicable), OpCode, users last logged-on date and time, task category, keywords (audit success or fail) and the computer name. The event information can be copied by clicking on *Copy* button (located at left-bottom of the *Event Properties* window) and copied information can be saved into a word document file for future reference. Click on *Close* to exit out of the window.

Audited event information can be viewed in friendly view or in XML view, click the *Details* tab to select the *Friendly View* or *XML View*. Click the plus sign (*) to expand the *System* and *EventData* category to view detailed information of an event. To copy an event information, click on *Copy* button and paste into a word document file for future reference.

REGISTRY EDITOR

A *Registry Editor* is an administrator tool to manage hardware and software registry preferences. It stores system hardware settings, Microsoft and non-Microsoft software settings, local user and remote user's preferences, and preferences of a local machine. The *Registry Editor* is divided into a number of logical sections and it contains information of a local machine, currently logged-in users, currently installed registered applications, and hardware profile information.

OPEN REGISTRY EDITOR

To open *Registry Editor*, run command prompt (*Windows Key + R*) to type *regedit* in the search box and then click *OK*.

HKEY_CLASSES_ROOT

The *HKEY_CLASSES_ROOT* key is abbreviated as *HKCR*. This registry stores application file associations, file extensions, ActiveX, and plug-ins detail.

HKEY_CURRENT_USER

The *HKEY_CURRENT_USER* key is abbreviated as *HKCU*. It stores currently logged- in user profile settings. The configuration will apply to currently logged-in user profile. Each user keeps separate profile configuration settings.

HKEY_LOCAL_MACHINE

The *HKEY_LOCAL_MACHINE* key is abbreviated as *HKLM*. It stores local machine hardware configuration profile settings. The configurations apply to all users' profiles.

HKEY_USERS

The *HKEY_USERS* key is abbreviated as *HKU*. It stores users and programs configuration settings that include configuration settings of a screen saver, fonts and folder view preferences.

HKEY_CURRENT_CONFIG

The **HKEY_CURRENT_CONFIG** key is abbreviated as *HKCC*. It stores local machine current hardware profile configuration settings.

ADD USER PERMISSIONS

Open *Registry Editor*. From left navigation panel of the *Registry Editor*, click the registry tree folder. Navigate to a registry key file and then click on *Edit* menu to select the *Permissions* option.

To specify everyone (for all users) permission, click on *Everyone* from the **Group or user names** box and then set appropriate permission rules from the *Permissions for Everyone* section. To set special permissions or advanced user permissions, click on *Advanced*.

In the *Permissions* tab, you, as a system administrator, have option to modify, remove, and add permissions for standard users. To add a new user, click on *Add*.

To set active local user permission, type a username in the search box to check the validity of an existing active user and then click *OK*. In the *Permissions level* dialog box, go through the permissions level to set appropriate active user permissions. Click *OK* to save user's preferences.

AUDIT SYSTEM REGISTRY

Open *Registry Editor*. From left side of the registry tree, click the registry key file which needs to be audited. Make sure a registry key is selected and then click on *Edit* menu to select the *Permissions* option. Click on *Advanced* button. Click the *Auditing* tab and then click on *Add* button.

Enter the name of a user that needs to be audited in the search box and then click *OK*. If you, as a system administrator, have entered a correct username, you will be prompt to the permission level window that will allow you to audit successful and failed user log-on attempts to create, delete, and modify system registry key settings otherwise you will be asked to correct the username to continue the process.

In the *Auditing Entry* dialog box, select an appropriate audit level from the *Access* box and then click *OK* to save user's auditing preferences.

REGISTRY KEY OWNER

Open *Registry Editor*. From left side of the registry tree, click the registry key which user would like to take ownership. Make sure desired registry key is selected and then click on *Edit* menu to select the *Permissions* option. To add a new registry key owner, click on *Advanced* button.

In the *Owner* tab, click on *Other users or groups* button to add another owner. Enter new registry key owner name in the search box which needs permission to modify, delete, and create new system registry keys within the registry folder. Click *OK* to save preferences. Click on *Apply* and then click *OK* to save registry settings.

OWNERSHIP EFFECTIVE PERMISSIONS

Open *Registry Editor*. From left side of the registry tree, click the registry key to view and manage effective permissions. To manage and view the effective permissions, click on *Edit* menu to select *Permissions* option. Click on *Advanced* button. Click the *Effective Permissions* tab and then click on *Select*.

Enter an owner username that is previously associated with this registry. Click *OK* to view the effective permissions.

ADD REGISTRY KEY

To create a new registry key, go to *Edit* menu, click *New* and then click the *Key* to create a new system key.

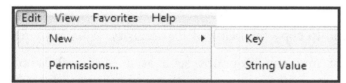

Image 4.6: Registry Key Edit Menu

FIND REGISTRY KEY

Open *Registry Editor* and then highlight the name of the registry key that user would like to search. For example, if user would like to search local machine registry key, user must click on *HKEY_LOCAL_MACHINE* registry name and then click on *Edit* menu to select *Find* option to open *Search* dialog box.

In the *Search* dialog box, type a desire registry key name and then click on *Find Next*. If user would like to find more similar registry key values, either go to *Edit* menu to select the *Find Next* option or press *F3* key (from a keyboard) to find next registry value.

PRINT REGISTRY KEY

From left navigation panel of the *Registry Editor*, click the registry tree folder and then navigate to a registry key file which user would like to print. For example, if user wants to print off a registry key named *HKEY_CURRENT_CONFIG* select the registry name and go to the *File* menu to choose *Print* option. If user has multiple printers installed on a machine, select the correct printer device from the *Select Printer* section and then click on *Print* button to print that registry key.

COPY KEY NAME

From left navigation panel of the *Registry Editor*, choose the name of a registry folder that user would like to copy. For example, if user wants to copy the name of the *HKEY_LOCAL_MACHINE* registry select the registry name and then select the *Copy Key Name* option from the *Edit* menu to copy the name of that registry. After copying the registry name, user can paste it into any programs such as a Microsoft Word document, a notepad, etc for later use.

ADD FAVORITES TO REGISTRY EDITOR

From left navigation panel of the *Registry Editor*, select a registry name that user would like to add to the *Registry Editor* Favorites. For example, if user wants to add the *HKET_CLASSES_ROOT* registry to favorites, click on it and then click on *Favorites* menu from registry menu bar and then select the *Add to Favorites* option to add it to the *Registry Editor Favorites*. Click on *OK* to add registry name to the favorite's folder.

REMOVE REGISTRY KEY FROM FAVORITES

To remove a registry name from favorites, go to the *Favorites* menu and then choose the *Remove Favorites* option to remove the registry name from the *Registry Editor Favorites*. Highlight the registry name that needs to be removed from *Select Favorite(s)* box and then click *OK*. To view *Registry Editor Favorite's* list, click on *Favorites* menu.

EDIT REGISTRY KEY VALUE DATA

From left navigation panel of the ***Registry Editor***, click the registry tree folder and then navigate to a registry key that user would like to modify. Click the registry value from right navigation panel of the ***Registry Editor*** that user wants to modify and then go to the ***Edit*** menu to choose the ***Modify*** option. Enter a value data in the ***Value data*** field and then click on ***OK*** to save changes.

MODIFY REGISTRY KEY BINARY DATA

From left navigation panel of ***Registry Editor***, click a registry tree folder, navigate to a registry key that user would like to modify and then go to the ***Edit*** menu to select the ***Modify Binary Data*** option. Edit the binary value and then click on ***OK*** to save changes.

REMOTE DESKTOP

Remote Desktop Connection is designed for system administrators to remotely connect to a client machine from the remote machine to perform administrative tasks such as downloading and installing Windows updates and changing system configuration settings, if necessary.

To establish a connection to a host machine, both the host and the client machines must have:

- Internet connectivity
- ***Windows Firewall*** must be configured properly to allow communication through a ***Remote Desktop*** port.
- Administrators must have a valid computer account on a client machine to log-in remotely to perform administrative tasks.

Only an administrator or a member of an administrative group has privileges to change ***Remote Desktop*** settings.

OPEN REMOTE DESKTOP CONNECTION

Click the ***Start*** button to type ***Remote Desktop Connection*** in the search bar and then press ***Enter*** from the keyboard.

To establish a connection between a host and a client machine, user must type-in a valid remote IP address or a remote machine name in the provided search field. A secure port needs to be added in front of the IP address if connecting to a secure remote system.

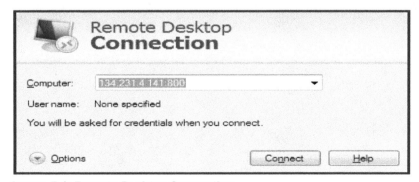

Image 5.1: Remote Desktop Connection

ESTABLISH REMOTE DESKTOP CONNECTION

Open *Remote Desktop Connection* window. Type an IP address of the remote computer in the search bar and then click on *Connect*. A connection from a host machine to a remote machine will be established.

To authenticate a remote session, enter the username and password of the remote computer to validate a session. If remote connection is established successfully you (as a system administrator) will have full control over the client's PC to perform maintenance, troubleshoot technical issues, copy, delete, and modify user settings of the remote computer.

REMOTE DESKTOP OPTIONS

In the *Remote Desktop Connection* dialog box, click *Options* to adjust settings. The *Remote Desktop Connection* settings are explained below.

In the *General* tab, under the *logon settings* section, enter the remote computer name or an IP address of the remote computer and then click on *Connect*. User will be asked to provide administrative credentials to authenticate the remote session.

The current connection settings can be saved as a RDP (*Remote Desktop Protocol*) file on a local hard-disk by clicking on *Save* button (located under the *Connection settings* section).

In the *Display* tab, remote desktop connection size and color scheme can be adjusted to improve remote connection speed. In the *Remote desktop size* section, drag the slider right or left to maximize or minimize the remote desktop size, respectively.

To set *Remote Desktop Connection* color scheme, choose one of the available color options from the *Colors* section. To display a remote connection in full screen mode, check *Display the connection bar when in full screen mode* option.

In the *Local Resources* tab, remote session preferences can be adjusted by customizing the remote computer sound settings, keyboard settings, a connection to the local devices and resources.

To adjust remote computer sound preferences, click on **Settings** button to select an available option. By default, keyboard is set to work in **only when using the full screen** mode but it can be changed to the one of the available options (**on this computer**, **on the remote computer**, and **only when using the full screen**) as needed.

System administrators must manage and adjust computer local devices and resources to perform necessary task remotely. If remote machine needs to be configured for printing and copying documents, select the **Printers** option from the **Local devices and resources** section to adjust printer settings. Then select the **Clipboard** option to copy documents from the client to the remote machine or vice versa.

To optimize **Remote Desktop Connection** performance, choose one of the following connection speeds. The connection speeds are:

- Modem 56 Kbps
- Low-speed broadband (256 kbps – 2 Mbps)
- Satellite (2 Mbps – 16 Mbps with high latency)
- High-speed broadband (2 Mbps – 10 Mbps)
- WAN (10 Mbps or higher with high latency)
- LAN (10 Mbps or higher)

The desktop environment can be adjusted by choosing one of following options.

- Desktop background
- Font smoothing
- Desktop composition
- Show window contents while dragging
- Menu and window animation
- Visual styles
- Persistent bitmap caching

To save **Remote Desktop Connection** settings, click the **General** tab and then click on **Save** button to save current **RDP** settings.

In the *Advanced* tab, server authentication settings and *Terminal Services Gateway* settings must be configured properly to maintain the integrity of a remote connection. A server authentication verifies the remote computer connection which may stop establishing an unauthorized connection between a host and a client machine. *Terminal Services Gateway* creates secure and encrypted connection as it uses *Remote Desktop Protocol* (RDP), port 3389, and *Hypertext Transfer Protocol over Secure Socket Layer* (HTTPS), port 443, together to establish a secure connection between the client machine and the server machine. The *RDP* 3389 is *Remote Desktop Connection* port and it can be blocked by *Windows Firewall* to enhance network security, if needed. The *HTTPS* 443 port provides an extra layer of security to transmit data through a *Secure Socket layer* (SSL) tunnel for TS Gateway to establish a secure network environment.

The *TS Gateway* server authentication method is designed for authorized users to establish a secure connection to a remote machine on a corporate network, if it is configured properly. Three options are available to choose to configure *TS Gateway Server*.

- *Connect and do not warm me if server authentication fails:* If *Remote Desktop Connection* cannot verify the identity of a remote computer, it still connects to the remote computer. This option is not recommended.

- *Warn me if authentication fails*: If *Remote Desktop Connection* cannot verify the identity of a remote computer, user will be notified to take necessary steps, if required, before connecting to the remote computer.

- *Don't connect if authentication fails*: If *Remote Desktop Connection* cannot verify the remote machine identity, the host machine will terminate connection immediately.

To configure *Remote Desktop Gateway* server settings, click the *Settings* from the *Connect from anywhere* section. By default, the client computer is configured to detect *RD Gateway* settings automatically.

To customize *RD Gateway server* settings, click the *Use these RD Gateway server settings* and then type server name in the *Server name* box. Select one of the following *Log-on methods*.

- *Allow me to select later:* At the time of connection, user selects a log-on method.

- *Ask for Password:* At the time of connection, a valid password is required to authenticate this session.

- *Smart Card:* At the time of connection, insertion of a smart card is required for authentication purpose to continue.

If the *RD Gateway server* authentication is not required, disable this feature by selecting the *Do not use a RD Gateway server* option and then click on *OK* to save changes. The *Remote Desktop Connection* works faster by clearing off the *Bypass RD Gateway server for local addresses* box.

REMOTE DESKTOP CONNECTION SETTINGS

To adjust *Remote Desktop Connection* settings, right-click on my *computer* icon to choose *Properties* option. From left navigation pane of the *System* window, click on *Remote settings* link. Select one of the following *Remote Desktop Connection* preferences.

- Don't allow connection to this computer

- Allow connections from computers running any version of Remote Desktop (less secure)

- Allow connections only from computer running Remote Desktop with Network Level Authentication (more secure)

Click on *Apply* and then click *OK* to save system settings.

ADD REMOTE DESKTOP LOCAL USER

To add a *Remote Desktop* local user, choose *Properties* option by right-clicking on *Computer* icon. From left navigation pane of the *System* window, click on *Remote settings* link. Click the *Remote* tab from the *Remote Desktop* section; click the *Select Users* to add users in that list.

Click on *Add* button to add a *Remote Desktop* user. Only existing or active local users are permitted to connect with this computer remotely.

From the *Select Users* window, click on *Advanced* button and then click on *Find Now* to search active local users. Then select the local user that needs to be added to the *Remote Desktop Group*. The *remote desktop group* members can connect to this computer remotely. Click *OK*.

WINDOWS REMOTE ASSISTANCE

Windows 7 users allow trusted users to manage or troubleshoot a system by taking control of a user machine remotely. The client and the remote user must have internet connection to accept remote assistance invitation. Assistance from trusted users can be asked by sending an invitation file using *Windows Mail*, if it is configured properly. Otherwise send the invitation file as an attachment using other email vendors, e.g., Google mail, Yahoo mail, Hotmail etc.

An administrator or a member of an administrative group has privileges to configure *Remote Assistance* settings.

OPEN WINDOWS REMOTE ASSISTANCE

To open *Windows Remote Assistance*, click the *Start* button to type *Windows Remote Assistance* in search bar and then press *Enter* from the keyboard.

REMOTE ASSISTANCE SETTINGS

To open *Remote Assistance* window, right-click on the *Computer* icon to select the *Properties* option from the list. From left navigation pane of the *System* window, click on *Remote settings* link. To allow a remote assistance connection to this computer, click the *Remote* tab. From the *Remote Assistance* section, select the *Allow Remote Assistance connections to this computer* option in order to get remote assistance request from other users.

To adjust *Remote Assistance* advanced settings, click on *Advanced* button. An authorized user may control client machine remotely if *Allow this computer to be controlled remotely* option listed under the *Remote control* section is enabled. To set maximum time limit for an invitation to remain open, adjust the invitation time from the *Invitation* section.

To seek assistance from *Windows Vista* users or later operating system users only, check the *create invitations that can only be used from computers running Windows Vista or later* option from the *Invitations* section and then click *OK* to save changes.

USER ACCOUNTS

Microsoft *Windows 7* users may create a standard user account and/or create an administrator account on a local machine or on a remote machine. A standard user account has limited privileges to change system settings; on the other hand, an administrator account has full rights to manage user's accounts and their profile settings. To modify, delete, and manage user's accounts, user must be a member of the administrative group or must have administrative privileges.

OPEN USER ACCOUNTS WINDOW

To open *User Accounts* window:

- Open *All Control Panel Items*
- Double-click *User Accounts*

System administrators perform necessary tasks such as changing user's passwords, removing user's passwords, changing user's profile picture, changing user's account types, re-naming user's accounts, turning on or off UAC (User Account Control), managing user's credentials, creating a reset password disk, managing network password and file encryption certificates to maintain the integrity of a standard user account.

SETUP USER ACCOUNTS

Open *User Accounts* window. From right navigation pane of the *User Accounts* window, click the *Manage another account* link to manage local user's accounts. A user account must be created in advance to access local or network resources (e.g., Pictures, Files & Folders, and Documents, etc) of a machine. A local user account is created for a specific machine and for a specific user.

A new local user account can be created by clicking on *create a new account* link. To create a new user account:

- Type a unique user's account name.
- Select one of the available account types, either a *standard user* or *administrative* group.
- Click *Create Account* to create a new user account.

The two types of user accounts are:

Standard Account: A standard user account has permission to run most programs. It has limited privileges to install and modify hardware and software profile settings. User may change system settings that do not affect other users profile settings or security of a system.

Administrator Account: It is a privileged account that performs all administrative tasks such as creating and managing local user's accounts, changing hardware and software configurations to make system performance better, and restricting users to modify hardware and software profile settings to maintain the security of a system.

CHANGE USER ACCOUNT TYPE

Open *User Accounts* window. From right navigation pane of the *User Accounts* window, click the *Change your account type* to change local user account type. Select an account type (a *standard user* or an *administrator*) and then click the *Change Account Type*.

CHANGE USER ACCOUNT PASSWORD

Open *User Accounts* window. From right navigation pane of the *User Accounts* window, click the *Change your password* link to manage a local user's password.

To set a new user account password:

- Type the current password
- Create new account password
- Confirm the new password
- Click on *Change password* to reset user's account password

REMOVE USER ACCOUNT PASSWORD

Open *User Accounts* window. From right navigation pane of the *User Accounts* window, click the *Remove your password* link to remove local user password. User will be asked to provide the current user's password and then click on *Remove Password* to remove current user account password.

REMOVE USER ACCOUNT

Open *User Accounts* window. From right navigation pane of the *User Accounts* window, click the *Manage another account* link to select a user account that needs to be removed. Select the *Delete the account* option to remove the user account.

You, as a system administrator, will be asked what needs to be done with the user's personal files. If you decided to keep the user's files, click on *Keep Files*. A folder will be created on computer desktop to save user's documents, favorites, music, pictures, and video files. If the user's files are not necessary to save, click on *Delete Files* to delete the user's account and user's personal data files. This process may take few minutes to delete the user account.

USER ACCOUNT CONTROL

A *User Account Control* (UAC) security feature adds an extra layer of security to minimize risk of installing malicious codes into a user system.

To adjust the *UAC* settings, open *User Accounts* window. From right navigation pane of the *User Accounts* window, click the *Change User Account Control settings* link to change local *User Account Control* settings.

The *UAC* preferences can be set by moving slider up and down.

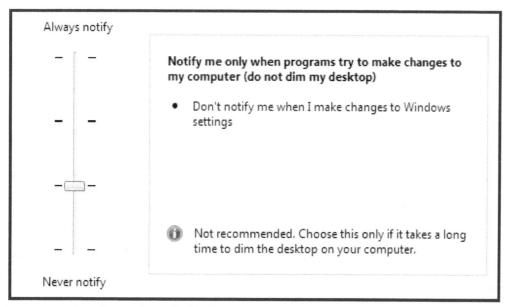

Image 5.2: User Account Control Settings

ADVANCED USER ACCOUNT PROPERTIES

To manage user accounts and their passwords, open advanced user account properties window. Click on *Start* button to type *netplwiz OR control userpasswords2* in the search bar and then click *OK* to launch advanced user account properties window.

An administrator can add new user accounts, remove existing user accounts, and reset user passwords. Click on *Apply* and then click *OK* to save changes.

LOCAL AREA NETWORK

A local area network covers a small geographical area such as your home, an office, and a school. The connectivity of the connection is limited to a single building or group of buildings. An administrator or a member of administrative group has privileges to modify local area network settings.

OPEN NETWORK SHARING CENTER

To open *Network Sharing Center*:

- Click *Start* button
- Click *Control Panel*
- Click **Network** *and Internet*
- Click *Network and Sharing Center*

VIEW LOCAL AREA NETWORK STATUS

Open *Network and Sharing Center*. From right navigation pane of the *Network and Sharing Center*, click the *Wireless Network Connection* (if user connected through a wireless adaptor) or click the *Local Area Connection* (if user connected through a wired Ethernet cable) from *View your active networks* section to see the connectivity of a local connection.

A *Local Area Connection Status* window shows: the connection speed, duration of connection time, media status, IPV4 connectivity status, IPV6 connectivity status, and data packets statistics that being sent by the router and received by the computer. Click on *Close* after done reviewing the local area connection status information window. The network connection details can also be viewed by clicking on *Details* button from the *Connection* section.

DISABLE LOCAL AREA NETWORK CONNECTION

Open *Local Area Connection Status* window. In the *General* tab, from the *Activity* section, click the *Disable*.

If the local area network connection is disabled, a **Red Cross Mark** ⊞ will appear on the computer icon in the system tray (located at right-bottom of a computer desktop).

ENABLE LOCAL AREA NETWORK CONNECTION

Open *Network and Sharing Center*. In the *Network and Sharing Center* section, a *Red Cross Mark* on a line that connects the user computer to the Internet indicates no connectivity between user computer and a network. There are many possible reasons of not having connectivity between two devices. The most common reason is disabled of a network card. To enable a network card, click the *Change Adapter settings* link from left navigation pane of the *Network and Sharing Center*.

Image 5.3: Connection between this computer and Internet

From *Network Connections* window, right-click on the disabled local area network connection to select the *Enable* option from the list. If system has both wireless and wired network connections available, user may see multiple local area network connections.

Image 5.4: Local Area Connection

Now, the local area network connection is enabled and it has connectivity to it. A local area network icon will appear in notification area (located at right-bottom of the desktop).

CHANGE NETWORK LOCATION TYPE

From right navigation pane of the *Network and Sharing Center* window, click either *Home Network* or *Public Network* or *Work Network* link from *View your active networks* section to select a network location type. Select a preferred network location type and then click *Next*.

There are three network location types (*Home, Work, and Public*) are available to adjust a network location type. Both *Home* and *Work* are trusted networks. A public network works in public area such as an airport, a coffee shop, and at unsecure places where a security key is not required connecting to the Internet because this service is available to public for free of charge. A private network is more secure network type such as your home or office network. Also, it is known to be more secure network which passes encrypted communication across the network. If a user is concered of his computer security, private network will be the best choice for the user machine. If the network location type is set successfully, user will be notified. Click on *Close* to exit out of the window.

IP ADDRESS AND DNS SERVER CONFIGURATION

IP stands for *Internet Protocol*. To share computer resources across the network, every computer requires to have a unique IP address. The IP addresses, subnet mask, default gateway, and other IP parameters for a home user is assigned automatically. *Dynamic Host Configuration Protocol* (DHCP) server needs to be installed for domain users to get IP address for their systems. This method helps system administrators to manage and control IP addresses over the network.

A *Dynamic Name System* (DNS) translates hostnames into IP addresses to deliver that information to network equipments that are only capable of understanding IP addresses, not hostnames. For example, www.yahoo.com is a hostname and it is only understandable by human beings, not by network equipments such as computers, servers, routers, and switches. To establish a communication session between human beings and network equipments, we need to know the IP address of the hostname. The IP address of the yahoo website is 69.147.76.15 and it needs to be sent to the network equipment to establish a successful communication session.

To configure IP address and a DNS server:

- Open *Network and Sharing Center*.
- Click the *Change Adapter settings* link from left navigation pane of *Network and Sharing Center*.
- From the *Network Connections* window, right-click on the local area network connection to choose *Properties* option from the list to configure IP address and a DNS server.

There are two Internet protocols (*IPV4* and *IPV6*) available for Windows 7 users. The *IPV4* are 32-bit address and *IPV6* are 128-bit group of 8 hexadecimal characters. To configure any of these Internet protocols, select the appropriate protocols from dialog box and then click on *Properties* button to type a correct IP address and a DNS server to configure a network device.

SHARED RESOURCES

Network user's shares resources via a local area network or a wide area network. A local area network covers a small geographical area such as your home and an office. A wide area network covers a large geographical area such as a state, a province, or a country.

SHARE FOLDER WITH A LOCAL USER

To share a folder with a local user:

- Right-click on a folder that user wish to share with a local user and then choose the *Properties* option from the list. To enable network sharing, click the *Sharing* tab from the *Folder Properties* window, under the *Network File and Folder Sharing* section, click on *Share*.
- Type a user name that needs permission to access shared folder over the

network and then click on *Add* button. The local user accounts must be created in advance to share network resources.

- Click on *Share* button to enable local user to have access to the shared resources over the network.

- Now, the local user is permitted to access the shared folder. A shared folder path is created to share with other local users as needed. Click on *Done* to end file sharing (e.g., pictures, documents, etc) process.

FILE AND PRINTER SHARING

The *File and Printer* sharing is a way to share printer resources across the network. File sharing happens between network users to transfer files across the network. This method may slow down network traffic if large files are in process to download. If file sharing happens between two network users where a files server is not involved such file sharing is called *peer-to-peer* sharing.

The network users must be configured properly to share resources. Open *Network and Sharing Center* window. From left navigation panel of the *Network and Sharing Center* window, click on *Change Advanced Sharing Settings* to configure file and printer sharing settings. Click the toggle arrow 🔽 to adjust (either a *public* or a *Home* or an *Office)* network and then scroll down to the file and printer sharing section.

To turn on file and printer sharing, click the *Turn on file and printer sharing* option and then click on *Save Changes* to save file and printer sharing preferences. An authorized user must have a username and a password to log on to the network to access shared files and printer resources.

FILE SHARING CONNECTION

Windows 7 uses 128-bit encryption method to protect file sharing connections between local network users. By default, 128-bit encryption is enabled for Windows 7 users to protect file sharing connections. Some devices may not support 128-bit encryption, in that case, user must use 40- or 56- bit encryption. The 40- or 56 bit encryption can be enabled by selecting *Enable file sharing for devices that use 40- or 56- bit encryption* option from *file sharing connections* section.

To turn on *File Sharing connections* feature, open *Network and Sharing Center*. From left navigation panel of the *Network and Sharing Center* window, click on *Change Advanced Sharing Settings*. Click on toggle arrow to select an appropriate option from the *File Sharing connections* section. Click on *Save Changes*.

PUBLIC FOLDER SHARING

By default, the public folder resides in *C* drive of *Users* folder. To access user public folder, Choose *Open Windows Explorer* option by right-clicking on *Start* button. Click on *Libraries* folder from left navigation panel to view public sharing folders. All network users have access to public folders if public folder sharing feature is active.

To enable public folder sharing feature, open *Network and Sharing Center*. From left navigation panel of the *Network and Sharing Center* window, click on *Change Advanced Sharing Settings*. Under the *Public folder sharing* section, click on *Turn on sharing so anyone with network access can read and write files in the Public folders* option to activate public folder sharing. Click on *Save Changes* to save public folder sharing preferences.

PASSWORD PROTECTED SHARING

A password protected sharing requires user to have a valid username and a valid password to authenticate user sessions to have access to share folders over the network. The network resources must be password protected.

To turn on *Password protected sharing* feature, open *Network and Sharing Center*. From left navigation panel of the *Network and Sharing Center* window, click on *Change Advanced Sharing Settings*. Choose the *Turn on password protected sharing* option from the *Password protected sharing* section. Click on *Save Changes* to save password protected sharing settings. It is recommended to enable password protected sharing feature to protect sharing resources over the network.

HOMEGROUP CONNECTIONS

HomeGroup connections can be managed manually or Windows 7 can manage *Homegroup* connection automatically if configured properly. It is recommended to let Windows to manage homegroup connection.

To manage a *homegroup* connection, open *Network and Sharing Center*. From left navigation panel of the *Network and Sharing Center* window, click on *Change Advanced Sharing Settings*. Select the *Allow Windows to manage homegroup connections (recommended)* option from *HomeGroup connections* section.

If user would like to manage and access a *Homegroup* connection by using a user account and a password that user has already setup to manage homegroup, choose *Use user accounts and passwords to connect to other computers* option. Click on *Save Changes* to save *Homegroup* connections preferences.

NETWORK DISCOVERY

A network discovery establishes a communication session between multiple network users to share computer resources and it also discovers other network devices across the network.

Network devices (such as a network computer and a router over the network) are not discoverable if the *Network discovery* is turned off. The network discovery must be turned on to discover other network resources.

To turn on *Network discovery* feature, open *Network and Sharing Center*. From left navigation panel of the *Network and Sharing Center* window, click on *Change Advanced Sharing Settings*. To activate network discovery feature, click on *Turn on network discovery* option from *Network discovery* section. Click on *Save Changes* to save network discovery preferences.

MEDIA SHARING

A media sharing happens between two or more network users to share media files across the network. The *Media Sharing* feature must be enabled to share media resources (e.g., shared music files, pictures, and video files, etc) across the network.

To start sharing media resources across the network, open *Network and Sharing Center*. From left navigation panel of the *Network and Sharing Center* window, click on *Change Advanced Sharing Settings*. Click on *Choose media streaming options* link from *Media sharing* section.

In the *Media Sharing* window:

- Type a media library name, and then

- Choose an appropriate network type (*local network* or *all network*s) option from drop down menu of *Show devices on*.

- User has an option to allow or block all shared media resources by clicking on *Allow All* or *Block All* button. Click *OK* to save media sharing preferences.

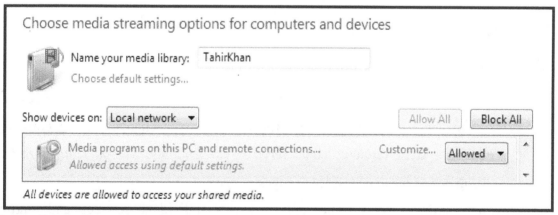

Image 5.5: Media Streaming Option

SYSTEM CONFIGURATION SETTINGS

A system configuration window is designed to allow system administrators to make appropriate changes with startup options, application services, and startup programs to troubleshoot a system.

OPEN SYSTEM CONFIGURATION WINDOW

To open system configuration window, run command line (*Windows Key + R*) to type *msconfig* in the search bar and then click *OK*. If user prompted for administrative credentials, provide credentials to continue.

User must understand computer startup options in detail to activate proper computer mode.

NORMAL STARTUP MODE

In normal startup mode, the system loads all device drivers and application services. By default, every system is set to start in normal mode to load all device drivers and application services.

DIAGNOSTIC STARTUP MODE

The diagnostic startup mode is design to load basic devices and services and it also checks corrupted Windows files to isolate a program or an application service which may be causing issues for a system to startup.

SELECTIVE STARTUP MODE

The available selective startup services are:

- *Load system services*: If this option is enabled, the system loads necessary system services to run system properly. To make changes to the currently running system services, click *Services* tab from the *System Configuration* dialog box to make necessary changes as needed.
- *Load startup items*: This option selects individual services and startup programs to isolate a program or a service that is causing problem for a system. To view the startup items list, click on *Startup* tab from the *System Configuration* dialog box.
- *Use original boot configuration*: If this option is enabled, the system startups with original boot configuration settings.

BOOT SYSTEM CONFIGURATION SETTINGS

To boot the system in *Safe Mode*, select *Safe Boot* option from *Boot options* section to isolate a computer startup issue. Restart system after selecting one of the following options.

The following boot system configurations settings must be checked properly to troubleshoot a computer issue.

- *Minimal*: System boots into the *Safe Mode*.

- *Alternate Shell*: Administrators make changes to a system using *DOS* command line.

- *Active Directory Repair*: System restores or repair *Active Directory* services.

- *Network*: User will have an access to Internet in safe mode.

- *No GUI boot*: If this option is disabled, system will boot faster than normal startup. At the startup of a computer, user may see a screen with the logo of Microsoft Corporation on it. This option will eliminate that screen to make system boot faster.

- *Boot Log*: This option stores system device drivers in the ntbtlog.txt file to isolate a device driver issue.

- *Base Video*: System will boot with basic display drivers to solve video resolution problem or other problems that are associated with a computer video card.

- *OS Boot Information*: Device drivers get display on startup screen.

- *Make All Settings Permanent*: All changes made to the boot configuration are marked permanent for all users.

APPLICATION SERVICES CONFIGURATION

It is recommended to disable application services which may be causing issues for a system to startup properly. To disable a service, click the *Service* tab to clear an appropriate *application service* checkbox from *System Configuration* window. Click on *Apply* and then click *OK* to save changes

STARTUP SERVICES

In the *Startup* tab, the startup items are listed with their names, their manufacture name, location of the startup items, and date they were disabled. The startup services are forced to start automatically every time user log-on to a system. User must disable unnecessary services to boot the system faster. For example, anti-virus and spyware programs are recommended at the startup of a system but all other services may be disabled to improve computer startup speed. To disable a startup item, clear an appropriate application checkbox and then click on *Apply* to save changes.

SYSTEM TOOLS

In the *Tools* tab, Microsoft has compiled a list of administrator management tools to launch an application by using the system configuration window. To launch a computer management tool, select an application that user would like to open and then click on *Launch* button. Click on *Apply* and then click *OK* to save changes.

GENERAL WINDOWS LOGO KEY SHORTCUTS

The Windows applications in table 6.1 can be launched with holding down the Windows logo key or the ALT/ CTRL key or the Shift key with the combination of another key.

Application Name	Keyboard Shortcuts
Display Windows Help	Windows logo Key + F1
Ease of Access Center	Windows logo Key + U
Lock the System or Log-off the System	Windows logo Key + L
Minimize All Open Applications	Windows logo Key + M
Run Dialog Box	Windows logo Key + R
Search Computer	Ctrl + Windows logo Key + F
Search Files and Folder	Windows logo Key + F
Show Desktop	Windows logo Key + D
Systems Properties Window	Windows logo Key + Pause/Break Key
Windows Explorer	Windows logo Key + E
3D-Flip	Windows logo Key + Tab
3D-Flip (Persistent)	Ctrl + Windows logo Key + Tab

Table 6.1: Windows Logo key Shortcuts

CONTROL KEY (CTRL), ALTERNATIVE KEY (ALT), SHIFT KEY, AND FUNCTION KEY SHORTCUTS

The Windows applications in table 6.2 can be launched with holding down the ALT key, CTRL key, or the Shift key with the combination of another key.

Application Name	Application Shortcuts
Bypass Recycle Bin for Deleted Items	Shift + Delete
Close Active Window	Alt + F4
Display Selected Folder Properties	Alt + Double-click
Find Files and Folder	F3
Move Through the Items	Tab
Refresh Active Window	F5
Rename a Selected Item	F2
Start Menu	Ctrl + Esc
Switch Between Open Applications	Alt + Tab
Windows Help and Support	F1
Windows Task Manager	Ctrl + Shift + Esc

Table 6.2: Keyboard Function keys Shortcuts

KEYBOARD SHORTCUTS

Windows applications mentioned in table 6.3 can be launched by typing a command line in the search filed (*Windows logo key + R*). To open an application, type one of the following command lines in the run dialog box and then click *OK* to launch the application.

Application Name	Application Shortcuts
Device Manager	Hdwwiz.cpl
Add/Remove Programs	Appwiz.cpl
Administrative Tools List	Control Admintools
Appearance Settings	Control Color
Application Services	Services.msc
Application Data Folder	%Appdata%
Calculator	Calc
Certificate Manager	Certmgr.msc
Character Map	Charmap
Command Prompt (DOS-Window)	CMD
Component Services	Dcomcnfg
Computer Management Console	Compmgmt.msc
Control Panel	Control Panel
Date and Time	Timedate.cpl
Direct X Diagnostic Tool	Dxdiag
Device Manager	Devmgmt.msc

Disk Cleanup Options	Cleanmgr
Disk Management	Diskmgmt.msc
Disk Partition Manager	Diskpart
Display/Monitor Settings	Desk.cpl
Driver Verifier Manager	Verifier
Event Viewer	Eventvwr.msc
Firefox Browser (If available)	Firefox
Folders Properties	Control Folders
Google Chrome Browser (If available)	Chrome
Group Policy Editor (If supported)	Gpedit.msc
Home Directory	%Homepath%
Home Directory Drive	%Homedrive%
IExpress Wizard	Iexpress
Internet Explorer Browser	Iexplore
Internet Properties	Inetcpl.cpl
Keyboard Properties	Control Keyboard
Local Security Settings	Secpol.msc
Local Users and Groups (If supported)	Lusrmgr.msc
Log-off	Logoff
Microsoft Excel Document (If supported)	Excel
Microsoft Outlook (If supported)	Outlook

Microsoft Paint	Mspaint or Pbrush
Microsoft PowerPoint	Powerpnt
Microsoft Synchronization Tool	Mobsync
Microsoft Word Document	Winword
Mouse Properties	Control Mouse
Network Connections	Control Netconnections
Notepad	Notepad
On-screen Keyboard	Osk
Phone and Modem Options	Telephon.cpl
Power Options	Powercfg.cpl
Printers and Faxes	Control Printers
Program Files and Folder	%Programfiles%
Regional and Language Options	Intl.cpl
Registry Editor	Regedit
Remote Desktop Connection	Mstsc
Restart a System	Shutdown –r
Shared Folders	Fsmgmt.msc
Shutdown a System	Shutdown
Sounds and Audio Properties	Mmsys.cpl
SQL Server Client Configuration	Cliconfg
System Configuration Editor	Sysedit

System Configuration Utility	Msconfig
System Information	Msinfo32
System Performance	Perfmon
System Properties	Sysdm.cpl
Task Manager	Taskmgr
Task Scheduler	Control Schedtasks
Temporary Folder	%Temp%
Windows Account Security	Syskey
Windows Address Book	Wab
Windows Address Book Import Utility	Wabmig
Windows Directory	%Windir%
Windows Easy Transfer Tool	Migwiz
Windows Firewall	Firewall.cpl
Windows Magnifier	Magnify
Windows Media Player	Wmplayer
Windows Narrator	Narrator
Windows Root Directory	%Windir%
Windows Root Drive	%Systemdrive%
Windows Security Center	Wscui.cpl
Windows Version	Winver

Table 6.3: Keyboard Shortcuts

NETWORK COMMAND-LINE UTILITIES

Command prompt (*DOS-Window*) configures *Internet Protocol* (IP) addresses as needed. System administrators often use command prompt window to resolve network issues by typing a suggested command line listed in table 6.4.

To open a command prompt window, open *Run* dialog box (*Windows logo key* + *R*) to type *CMD* in the search bar. Click on *OK* to open a *DOS-Window*.

Application Name	Application Command
Address Resolution Protocol Cache Table	Arp –a
Display DNS Cache	Ipconfig/displaydns
Display Connection Configuration	Ipconfig/all
Domain Name Server	Nslookup
Flush DNS Cache	Ipconfig/flushdns
Path Ping (IP Trace Utility)	Pathping [IP address of the host computer]
Ping the Client/Server Machine	Ping [IP address of the host/server]
Release all Network Connections	Ipconfig/release
Renew all Network Connections	Ipconfig/renew
TCP/IP Networking Statistics	Netstat
Windows IP Configuration	Ipconfig
End Currently Running Application	Ctrl +C

Table 6.4: Network Command-line Utilities

WINDOWS SYSTEM FILE COMMAND-LINE

Windows system files that are modified or altered by a third-party can be repaired by typing one of the following command lines in a DOS-window.

To open a DOS-window, open **Run** dialog box, type **CMD** in search bar and then click **OK** to open command prompt.

Application Name	Application Command
Scan Immediately	Sfc/scannow
Scan on Next Boot	Sfc/scanonce
Scan on Every Boot	Sfc/scanboot
Cancel Pending Scans	Sfc/cancel
Default System Settings	Sfc/revert
Purge File Cache	Sfc/purgecache
Set Cache Size	Sfc/cachesize = X (X represents any number)
Scans System Files	Sfc/verifyonly
Check Disk	Chkdsk
Locate and Recover Bad Hard-Drive Sectors	Chkdsk/r
Close Command Prompt	Exit
Stop Currently Running Processes	Ctrl + C

Table 6.5: Windows System File Command-line

144

www.ingramcontent.com/pod-product-compliance
Lightning Source LLC
Chambersburg PA
CBHW080421060326
40689CB00019B/4328